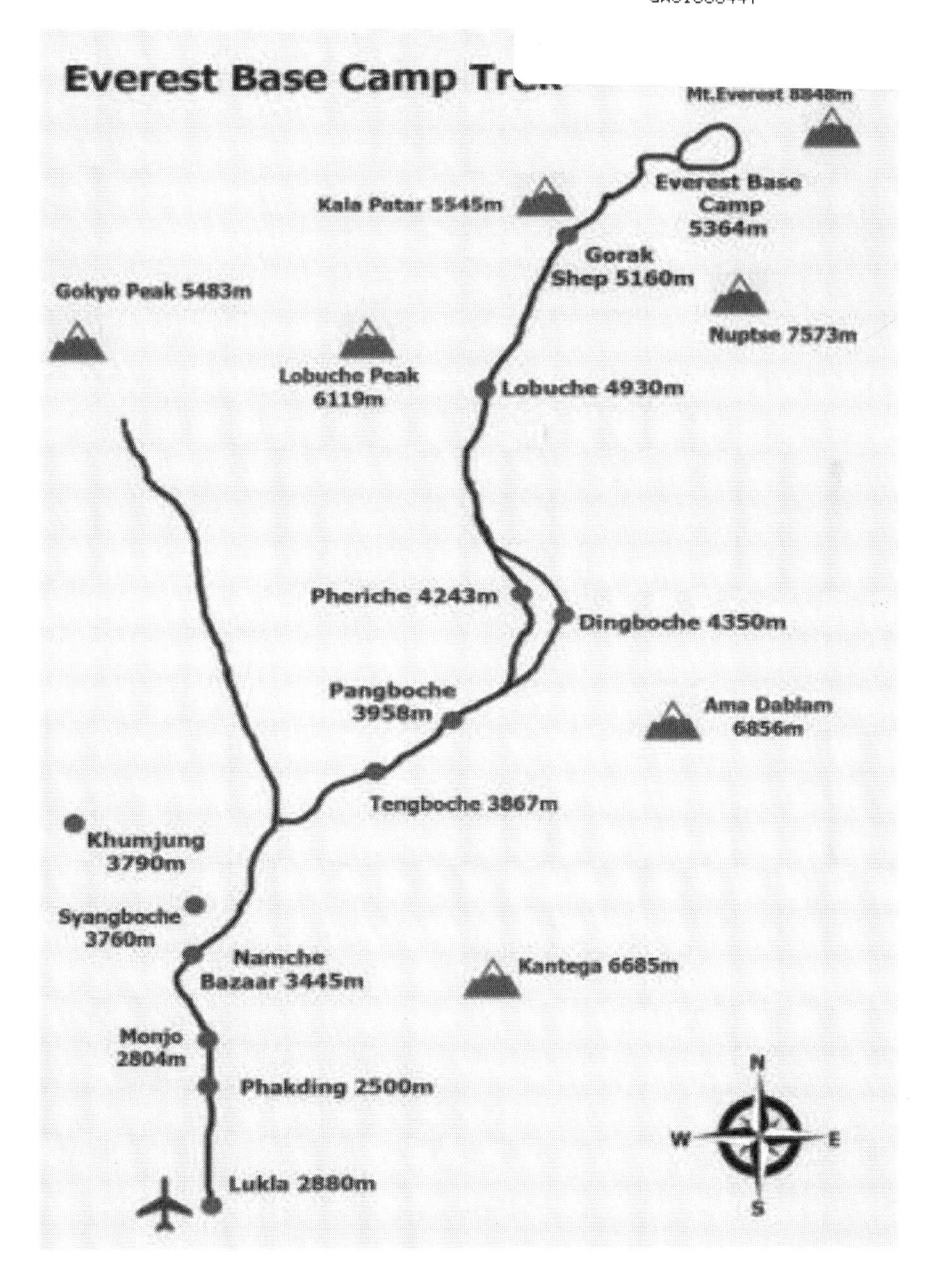

Everest Base Camp Trek

Stupa above Namche. Everest and Lhotse in the background.

WHERE IS IT AND WHAT IS IT?

Everest Base Camp (EBC) is positioned in a place of Nepal called the Khumbu region, Northeast of the capital, Kathmandu. Every yr from approximately March via May climbers from all around the global create and congregate in a makeshift camp wherein they slowly acclimatise in training for hiking the global's maximum mountain. For the relaxation of the yr the vicinity called Base Camp is only a mass of rocks and ice (on the give up of one of the maximum scenic hiking routes withinside the global). Base Camp is 5364 meters (17598 feet) above sea level. So even as now no longer pretty similar to hiking Everest, getting there's no stroll withinside the park. It is really well worth citing at this factor which you can not see Everest from Base Camp. While the pinnacle of the mountain may be visible from diverse factors alongside the way, for the excellent perspectives you want to ascend Kala Patar. Many humans pick out to do each, regularly factoring in a further day on their journey. It's feasible to do them withinside the equal day, however it's a tough push.

ABOUT ME

I am fairly properly travelled, in as plenty as I've been to many towns across the global. This is in particular due to my girlfriend, who loves traveling even extra than I do. Left to my very own gadgets it's dubious I'd were to 1/2 of the locations we've been together. What generally takes place is she indicates an area and I go with it. However in 2013 some thing changed. I realised that I didn't need to peer but any other city. I had all started to sense that, in spite of language and cultural differences, whilst it comes proper right all the way down to all of it towns are extra or much less the equal. I desired some thing extra – surroundings – the kind of surprising surroundings I'm constantly seeing photographs of online. With that during thoughts we determined to visit Peru and booked a bundle deal that protected a 3 day trek at the Lares trail. Neither folks had finished any hiking before. And this became what you may call 'luxurious hiking', a coddled excursion that protected a guide, a prepare dinner dinner and a porter, in addition to mules to hold our gear, tents and cooking facilities. I'm a bit embarrassed to confess that now, however I must confess it became an extraordinary experience, in particular due to our informed and amiable guide, Maritza, who nursed us each step of the way. Nevertheless, our brief trek in Peru became some thing of a surprise to each our systems. We suffered altitude illness and have been breathless plenty of the time, in spite of spending numerous days acclimatising in Cusco. The climate wasn't precisely type either, with plenty of the surroundings obscured via way of means of mist and rain. At one factor we discovered ourselves in what via way of means of Peruvian requirements became likely a slight snowstorm, however to us felt like a raging blizzard. Slowly ascending, preventing each 5 steps to gasp for breath, I recollect questioning I might in no way ever try to do something like this once more so long as I lived! And but… upon of of entirety all I felt became a feel of achievement. How tough it have been fast diminished from memory. I had stuck the hiking computer virus and couldn't wait to head once more.

The following yr noticed Janet and I head to the wilds of Patagonia wherein I stumbled upon a ee-e book known as 'Into Thin Air' via way of means of Jon Krakauer. This will be the starting of my fascination with all matters Everest, and brought on my selection to visit Everest Base Camp a yr later. For every body strange with the tale right here it's miles in a nutshell (WARNING: SPOILERS).

INTO THIN AIR

In 1996 journalist/climber Jon Krakauer became commissioned via way of means of Outside
mag to climb Everest with an excursion agency known as Adventure

Consultants, owned via way of means of New Zealand guide, Rob Hall. His remit became to evaluate the effect business expeditions have been having at the mountain. Professional climbers and different purists have been starting to bitch that such expeditions have been turning Everest right into a traveler vacation spot for the wealthy; folks that had slightly placed a foot on a mountain of their lives, motive on bagging the global's maximum height in simple terms for bragging rights. Stories have been filtering out of Base Camp of some 'clients' having to be proven the way to placed on a couple of crampons.

At the equal time, rival agency Mountain Madness, owned via way of means of Seattle primarily based totally Scott Fischer, became making its debut at the mountain, competing for commercial enterprise withinside the an increasing number of profitable business excursion sphere. Both events made their summit bids on May 10th, calculated to be one of the few climate home windows that make hiking Everest feasible. An sudden storm,
mixed with a sequence of errors and misfortunes, culminated withinside the deaths of 8 humans. The loss of life toll protected 3 Indian climbers ascending from the Tibetan facet of the mountain in what turned into, at that time, Everest's worst day (it has lately been closely surpassed).

Jon Krakauer made it out alive and, in addition to writing his piece for the magazine, went onto write his arguable ee-e book. Controversial due to the fact each time loss of life is concerned blame is apportioned and a few who have been there (and a few who weren't) selected to disagree with Krakauer's evaluation of what took place. Further books were written surrounding the occasions however none have come near shooting the spirit or the lousy tragedy that opened up in addition to 'Into Thin Air'. This can be due to Krakauer's journalistic eye for element or clearly due to the fact he's a extraordinary creator who can take any concern and make it study like a thriller. I am now no longer the primary character to be smitten with the aid of using his books and likely won't be the last. Krakauer additionally authored 'Into The Wild', made right into a movie of the equal call with the aid of using director Sean Penn. This chronicled the journey of backpacker, Christopher McCandless, who gave away his cash and went off to live to tell the tale withinside the Alaskan wilderness. The ee-e book has stimulated many younger humans to do the equal, endeavouring to retrace McCandless' footsteps, with a number of them finishing up the equal manner he did – dead. As lots as I loved that ee-e book, I'm satisfied to say 'Into Thin Air' captured my creativeness greater. As every other trekker stated to me once I instructed him why I'd come to EBC – "You've been Krakauered". It's greater not unusualplace than you'd think.

So, in addition to an possibility to move hiking in one of the international's maximum jaw losing destinations, my EBC trek turned into a pilgrimage to 'Into Thin Air', the tale that grew to become me into an Everest junkie and set me at the route to devouring books, now no longer best approximately Everest, however mountaineering in general; introducing me to a international of mad souls who always positioned their lives on the road at the same time as witnessing their pals die all round them yr after yr. I am no toward knowledge the psychology of such humans now as once I started. Nor, I'm satisfied to say, have I the slightest preference to climb a mountain. Upon commencing I was hoping now no longer best to make it to Base Camp however to live a night time there, if I ought to – to revel in a small piece of the Everest that climbers revel in. I had no concept if it turned into possible, as I wasn't proceeding on bringing a tent only for one night time – God is aware of I had sufficient to carry. I turned into additionally torn whether or not to move withinside the foremost hiking season while the climate might provide higher views, or withinside the mountaineering season while Base Camp might be thronging with climbers. But that turned into nonetheless 9 months away. In the give up I couldn't wait.

In 2015 the tale of the 1996 Everest catastrophe turned into made into the imaginatively titled Hollywood movie 'Everest', starring Jake Gyllenhall as Scott Fischer. I went to peer it earlier than I left. It failed spectacularly to seize the components that made the ee-e book one of these success. Leaving the cinema I ought to by no means have imagined that alongside the trek I might meet Scott Fischer's grown up children, who didn't just like the ee-e book or the movie.

SOME QUICK FACTS ABOUT EVEREST

- At 8848m (29,029 ft) above sea level the summit of Mount Everest is the highest place on Earth.

- The Nepalese name for the mountain is Sagarmatha, (Goddess of the sky), while Tibetans know it as Jomulungma (Goddess, mother of the world). In 1865, at the suggestion of Andrew Waugh, (British Surveyor General of India, tasked with calculating the height of the mountain), the Royal Geographical Society decided to name the mountain Everest after Waugh's predecessor in the role, Welsh surveyor and geographer - Colonel Sir George Everest. While that may have been extremely charitable of Waugh, it's believed Sir George, whose name was actually pronounced

Eve-rest, (emphasis on 'Eve') by no means noticed the mountain not to mention step foot on it, and objected to his call being used.

- Climbers who die on the mountain usually remain there forever due to the difficulty and enormous risk entailed in getting them down. Some make it their express wish that their bodies be left there, if they should perish. Often described as an open graveyard, Everest is home to the earthly remains of nearly 300 climbers. Most of these are in the Death Zone, above 8000m, where oxygen is about a third of what it is at sea level. Some of the corpses are used as markers, helping steer climbers towards the summit. Others are consumed by crevices, disappearing beneath the ever-shifting ice, never to be found.

- The process of climbing Everest is a long and laborious one. Climbers must spend weeks acclimatising their bodies to prepare for summit day, in order to lessen the risk of extreme altitude sickness that could result in death. A series of camps are assembled above Base Camp, to which climbers will make several excursions, going a little higher each time. Each excursion entails crossing the notorious Khumbu Icefall, full of gaping crevices as well as hidden ones that open up without warning. Large ice-blocks, some the size of ten-story buildings, loom precariously above and the danger of avalanches is prevalent. Many climbers have died here, the unmarried largest lack of lifestyles being on 18th April 2014, while 16 Sherpas perished in an avalanche at the same time as making ready the route.

- More climbers die while descending, after having summited, than going up.

- The first climbers to successfully ascend Everest were Edmund Hilary and Tenzing Norgay, reaching the summit at 11.30am on 29th May 1953.

- Most climbers use supplemental oxygen when making a bid for the summit. The first ascent without using supplemental oxygen was made by legendary Italian born mountaineer, Reinhold Messner in 1978, along side Peter Habeler. This turned into idea not possible on the time and lots of Sherpas refused to trust the pair's claim. Two years later Messner made the primary solo ascent of the mountain, once more with out supplemental oxygen.

- The risk of avalanche is highest during the day, when the heat of the sun causes the ice to melt. Hence those making their summit bids from Camp Four leave late at night, usually around 11pm to arrive on the summit the following day.

- The record for most successful ascents of Everest is jointly held by Sherpas, Phurba Tashi and Apa Sherpa who have summited the mountain an astonishing 21 times.

- Climbing Everest costs big money. An individual permit costs $11,000. Going with an excursion business enterprise can value between
$30 000 and $eighty five 000 For an in depth breakdown of prices visit:

- In April 2015 the earthquake that struck Nepal triggered an avalanche that swept through Base Camp, killing 18 mountaineers and their support staff.

- Everest is thought to rise by at least 4mm every year due to plate tectonics.

It's not all ice and snow-capped mountains.

WHY EVEREST BASE CAMP?

There are some of motives why humans desire to visit Everest Base Camp. Here are some I've come across.

- Everest Base Camp trek is much more than just a thoroughfare for mountain climbers. The breath taking scenery has made it one of the most popular destinations in Nepal. The word 'awesome' is highly overused these days but is truly appropriate when referring to the Everest Base Camp trek. You won't see anyone walking zombie-like with their head stuck in their phones around here.

- The culture. Trekking to EBC introduces you to the wonderful Nepali people and in particular the Sherpas, whose lives are so different from your own you can't really fathom it until you go there. If you've been born into Western civilization you might just realise how lucky you are, and might think twice before complaining how hard your job is in future!

- The challenge. Some people choose to run a marathon; others choose to trek to Everest Base Camp. Trekking to EBC will push any normal person to their physical limits. You will feel strengthened and empowered each step of the way and an incredible sense of achievement upon completion.

- Bragging rights. I'm far too modest to derive any benefit from this, but a lot of people like to be able to say they've been.

Sherpas carrying heavy loads

GETTING THERE

Getting there includes flying first to Tribhuvan International Airport in Kathmandu then taking a 30-minute flight to Lukla, in which the path begins. Those with masses of time on their fingers can pick out as a substitute to start the trek at Jiri, the unique direction to Everest utilized by early mountaineers earlier than Lukla's Tenzing-Hilary Airport turned into constructed in 1954. This will upload every other 8 to 9 days onto the trek and (I'm instructed with the aid of using a few who've performed it) quite a few needless hassle onto an already tough trek. The good sized majority of trekkers understandably pick out to start their trek at Lukla.

The flight to Lukla leaves from the home a part of the Tribhuvan International, quite simply positioned across the returned of the primary airport building. It is not likely you would need to get off the aircraft in Kathmandu and at once hop on every other to Lukla (even in case you could), so that you will absolutely be spending at the least one night time in Kathmandu. The vicinity in which the good sized majority of tourists/backpackers live is known as Thamel. It is a chaotic and interesting twenty-minute taxi journey from the airport into the thrashing coronary heart of Thamel. If for any cause you have to arrive and not using a coins and no lodging coated up, relaxation confident you'll locate an ATM and a hotel/hostel to live in inside mins of arrival. They are everywhere.

WHEN TO GO

February – May

This is seemed as the second one first-rate time of 12 months to go. The temperature is pleasantly heat and the rhododendrons are in complete bloom. The bonus of moving into May is it's additionally the hiking season, whilst mountaineers are at Base Camp. I've heard they don't precisely roll out the crimson carpet for trekkers, as they're paranoid you'll byskip in your germs and doubtlessly jeopardise their summit attempts. Which is comprehensible given how a great deal they've paid to be there.

June – August

This is the monsoon season and, in addition to being too warm to trek, it is able to regularly rain all day. I honestly wouldn't suggest going right now. Think mud- slides, being soaked thru, no perspectives and hardly ever another trekkers to percentage your distress with.

September – October

Most skilled trekkers experience that is the first-rate time of 12 months to visit Base Camp, as it's dry and the climate mild. I went in October and that's precisely the way it turned into. There have been clean perspectives for a great deal of the day. While from time to time clouds might come down and difficult to understand the perspectives it turned into hardly ever sufficient to experience you'd been cheated. At better altitudes the temperature extraordinarily drops, especially at night time whilst it is able to be underneath freezing.

November – January

This is wintry weather in Nepal, in which temperatures withinside the better areas can drop to as low as -30. Unless you simply revel in ache or are as difficult as hell don't even do not forget it. That said, others have performed it and loved a pretty extraordinary enjoy than maximum. However I'm now no longer going to suggest going solo right now of 12 months. It's additionally really well worth noting that many teahouses are close right now of 12 months. A bit like an English beach city in wintry weather.

HOW LONG DOES IT TAKE?

You actually need to permit your self sufficient time which you won't experience hurried. Two weeks off paintings is without a doubt now no longer going to be adequate. Including obligatory acclimatisation days, attending to EBC can take 9-10 days. From EBC returned to Lukla may be performed in as low as 2-3, as you do now no longer want to permit for acclimatisation and happening is manifestly a great deal quicker than going up, even if taking your time. You will want to feature onto that at the least one complete day in Kathmandu every aspect of your trek. As a minimal I might recommend scheduling sixteen days farfar from home – and that's reducing it fine.

To live pressure loose and get the maximum advantage from this trip, whilst bearing in mind viable illness and flight delays, you have to honestly permit your self 18 – 21 days. It have to be emphasized that seeking to do it quicker than this with the aid of using skipping acclimatisation days will significantly growth your probabilities of altitude illness and might jeopardise your whole journey.

WHERE WILL I STAY?

Three or 4 stone bathrooms withinside the village have been actually overflowing with excrement. The latrines have been so abhorrent that maximum people, Nepalese and Westerners alike, evacuated their bowels outdoor at the open ground, anyplace the urge struck. Huge stinking piles of human feces lay everywhere; it turned into not possible now no longer to stroll in it. The river of the snowmelt meandering thru the middle of the agreement turned into an open sewer. - Jon Krakauer, Into Thin Air

EBC is a teahouse trek, that means you don't want to carry a tent (until you in reality love camping). Nearly all teahouses (lodges) fee a hundred Nepalese rupees (approximately a dollar) for a room, supplied you devour there. Some fee as much as one thousand rupees in case you don't. They make their cash at the food, that's itself very moderately priced. There in reality isn't any motive why you wouldn't devour withinside the teahouse in which you're staying, as normally the handiest opportunity could be to move have dinner in some other teahouse with greater or much less the equal menu. And you'll in all likelihood be so worn-out you won't even don't forget going everywhere else. Rooms usually include unmarried beds, with pillows and blankets supplied (aleven though you need to nonetheless deliver an awesome slumbering bag).

Typical room in a teahouse.

Talk to anybody who stayed in a teahouse fifteen to 20 years in the past and they'll describe some thing corresponding to a barn with the door left open. Things have progressed fairly considering that then. Dormitories have made manner for rooms with dual beds. While now no longer precisely the Hyatt, teahouses are pretty cushty and offer all of the centers a coddled town kind may need, consisting of a sit-down toilet. It can get a touch bloodless withinside the evening, the handiest warmth being from the pot- bellied dung-burning stoves withinside the not unusualplace room. Many human beings want to huddle round these, however the warmth emanates out and it may even get a touch stuffy at times. It all offers the region a pleasant homely sense you simply can't get with

underfloor heating.

All teahouses offer hot (ish) showers. Like maximum different matters at the trek, the fee of a bath will increase with the altitude, however on common assume to pay more than one dollars.

Speaking of teahouses - tea fanatics be warned – in Nepal tea frequently comes with sugar already included. The Nepalese assume it peculiar that anybody could drink tea with out sugar, so in case you take yours with out, ensure you stipulate 'no sugar' whilst you order. On one event a lady laughed out loud once I asked this, like I changed into joking or some thing. On some other event the female serving stored making me repeat myself. The communication went some thing like:

Me: A cup of tea, please. No sugar.

Woman: (shocked): No sugar?

Me: Yes, no sugar, thanks.

Woman: No sugar?

Me: No, simply tea with out a sugar.

At which factor she grew to become to her pal and stated some thing in Nepalese which I interpreted as meaning: "Heh, get this – there's a few weirdo right here desires a cup of tea with out a sugar".

Stick the kettle on. Solar power is big in the Khumbu.

HOW FIT DO I NEED TO BE?

This changed into my largest fear earlier than going to Base Camp. I examine many tales of folks that were pressured to show round via now no longer being suit enough. A pal I bumped into informed me she had long gone with a set some years in the past and more than one infantrymen had given up and grew to become back! This didn't mainly fill me with confidence.

I hate workout of any sort. While hardly ever a sofa potato, I'm now no longer what you would possibly describe as a fantastically energetic character either. I play no sports, don't visit the health clubnasium and honestly don't jog (I attempted it as soon as however changed into fast triumph over through the tedium). I don't journey a bicycle and, to my shame, were recognized to force my automobile to the neighborhood shop, that's mins stroll from in which I live. Or as a minimum I did. One of the methods wherein Everest modified my lifestyles changed into that nearly at once upon returning I ditched the automobile and began out strolling everywhere. Oh – and I need to in all likelihood let you know I'm a smoker! That didn't change (I'm running on it). And yes, it'd have absolutely been an entire lot simpler if I wasn't a smoker. But I didn't permit it prevent me. Cigarettes or no cigarettes, hiking to Everest Base Camp changed into now no longer handiest doable, however fantastically

enjoyable. And for the time I changed into doing it as a minimum, my health stage increased, no matter myself. That stated it changed into absolutely the toughest bodily factor I've ever executed in my lifestyles. By the manner, I'm 50 years old. (There had been a number of human beings older than me at the trek. The oldest I noticed changed into a person in his seventies).

This may also appear unusual to a few, however the truth that I wasn't very healthy to start with made accomplishing Everest Base Camp sense even extra of an achievement. Not that I'm suggesting every body must really push aside the advantages of stepping into shape. However I strongly disagree with the bloggers who insist you must begin schooling 3 months earlier or you're going to be in for an lousy time and not able to experience the trek due to the fact you'll discover it the sort of struggle. I trust how an awful lot you experience it'll rely extra in your mind-set than whatever else. If you're out to interrupt velocity statistics then you definitely likely won't - and could be setting your self vulnerable to altitude illness. If you're taking all of the time you want, forestall while you want and as frequently as you want to take withinside the surroundings, chat to fellow trekkers, drink a few water or have a espresso at one of the many forestall-offs, you're assured to have a exquisite time. The villages are not so far apart that you're ever in any danger of not making it to the next one if you plan ahead – unless like me you're foolish enough to keep walking after dark and end up sleeping out in the hills (more about that later). There also are some of teahouses in among villages that frequently get neglected due to the fact maximum trekkers head directly for the following village wherein there are extra facilities.

The exceptional manner to teach for whatever is via way of means of doing it. The equal applies to hiking. Hill taking walks is a great concept however now no longer anyone has clean get admission to to a hill. So stairs or steps are an awesome alternative. If, like me, you're now no longer one for health regimes strive making small adjustments to your day by day lifestyles to growth your health level. Instead of straight away heading for the elevator take the steps instead. Leave the automobile at domestic and stroll to work. These little matters might not flip you right into a world-elegance athlete however they'll incrementally help in making ready you for what lies ahead.

Finally - consider hiking to Everest Base Camp as a manner of having healthy in itself, in your personal terms, whilst playing breath-taking surroundings and assembly a few amazing human beings alongside the manner. And undergo in thoughts that maximum those who fail to make it to Base Camp fail due to altitude illness or

intestinal troubles, now no longer health levels.

NOTE: I've study many locations you must keep away from caffeine whilst on EBC. I drank tea and espresso each day and didn't have any problems.

GROUP TREKKING

Going with a set charges plenty extra than going it alone. For your cash you get porters to hold your luggage (whilst you convey a mild daysack), a manual to take you there (whilst presenting certain nearby knowledge) and a set to percentage your joys and woes alongside the manner. If you do determine to go along with a set and are on a finances I could advocate reserving a set excursion in Thamel, slicing out the middlemen, whilst slicing down on charges and setting extra of your cash into the nearby economy. The notion of arriving in Kathmandu and looking for a hiking company may also appear a touch daunting for maximum human beings so get a listing of professional companies earlier than you leave. I will now no longer listing any right here as I don't have any non-public revel in of them however a short net seek will carry up dozens of pointers from individuals who have. Make certain your company is a member of TAAN (Trekking Agency of Nepal). An massive listing of members can be found on the TAAN internet site:

Once you've determined to go along with a set ensure to test what precisely is blanketed to your package deal and what isn't. Accommodation, meals, lets in and spherical journey flights from Lukla-Kathmandu are par for the course. You will nonetheless want to pay to your personal visas and journey coverage in addition to hiking equipment. A institution day trip will price among $1500 - $1800, which continues to be inexpensive than reserving thru a overseas primarily based totally company with a elaborate internet site and pictures of glad smiley human beings.

You will study some other place that one of the benefits of hiking with a set is that if whatever is going incorrect you're now no longer in your personal and could get hold of help in getting you decrease down or off the path completely. This can be true, however offers the impact that in case you're in your personal and some thing is going incorrect you're screwed. That is really now no longer the case. If you move throughout one of the hiking seasons the EBC trek is a hectic thoroughfare. You will now no longer wait very lengthy earlier than a person comes alongside, both different trekkers or Sherpas, who

Are inclined to assist. On more than one activities at the trek after I sat right all the way down to take a relaxation I became approached through neighborhood Sherpas supplying to hold my rucksack to my subsequent destination. On one of these occasion the guy was even going the opposite direction! Another man got really insistent to the point where I had to sit down longer than intended and tell him I would stay there all night rather than let him carry my rucksack. The factor is in case you get into problem there can be no scarcity of humans to assist. It's now no longer unbelievable that, if necessary, more than one Sherpas could assist get you and your rucksack to someplace wherein you may be helicoptered off – as many humans are every 12 months. This assumes you haven't been irresponsible sufficient to head with out acquiring an appropriate tour coverage and don't wander away the simply marked trek. In short, you shouldn't permit what may occur to steer your choice whether or not or now no longer to solo trek.

Hiring a Porter/Guide

An opportunity to going with a collection is to rent a manual and/or a porter. Fully certified courses do now no longer convey your bags aleven though there are porter/courses who will convey a few items. Most courses start out as porters and paintings their manner as much as turning into courses. Good courses can be capable of offer right neighborhood understanding that could make your journey extra exciting. If you're going to rent a manual make certain they may be skilled and may honestly upload fee on your journey. They have to communicate right English and be a person you locate exciting and smooth to get alongside with. Remember you will be spending approximately fourteen days on this person's company. I've skilled the pleasant and the worst of courses in numerous places, albeit for a restrained time – a tremendous manual who made a excursion of Rome's Coliseum one of the maximum memorable reviews ever, person who made Machu Picchu the dullest, any other in Rio de Janeiro who became under the influence of alcohol and disinterested and in reality admitted to me she didn't like humans, and of direction our Peruvian manual, Maritza, who became divine. I can't believe some thing worse than being caught with a terrible excursion manual for more than one hours not to mention a fortnight. And there's no purpose which you have to. For many humans having a remarkable excursion manual makes their enjoy unforgettable. For guidelines of neighborhood excursion courses attempt Trip Advisor.

NOTE: On my trek there have been memories flying round of trekkers being deserted through their courses, who have been in a hurry to get the trek completed with so they may get backtrack to Lukla to select out up extra clients. I met a Portuguese woman who I'm instructed this took place to. Our paths stored crossing on the primary day, from Lukla to Phakding then I by no means noticed her once more after that – which appears especially unbelievable if she had certainly carried on. It appears similarly not going that any Sherpa manual hired through a good organisation could behave this manner. I suspect that if that is in truth occurring then it's miles the 'courses' who loaf around Lukla airport supplying their offerings to trekkers upon arrival. As a precaution I could endorse simplest arranging thru a known organisation.

Expect to pay between $20-$30 in step with day for a manual and approximately $15 for a porter. This can range relying what time of 12 months you cross and may upward thrust throughout busy seasons.

The Case for Solo trekking

"The guy who is going on my own can begin today; however he who travels with any other should wait until that different is ready." – Henry David Thoreau

If 2015 is anything to go by and I had to hazard a guess at what percentage of trekkers go to Base Camp alone and unaided (including couples travelling without a guide) I would say five per cent - making you part of a very exclusive club. Here's what I suppose are the blessings of solo hiking over going with a collection or a manual.

- Cost. Going solo is cheaper by far. This will be the main consideration for most people. Why pay someone else for something you can do yourself? There are already enough occasions in life when paying for an expert is unavoidable and makes total sense. If you need to rewire a house you're going to need to hire an electrician. But you're not going to pay one to change a light bulb, are you? Going to EBC falls firmly in the category of things you can do yourself for a fraction of what it would cost to hire an expert.

- Independence and total freedom. You get to call the shots and go At your very own pace. While companies can also additionally vicinity a sturdy emphasis on going sluggish, the inescapable truth is you'll be going as sluggish as they need you to, now no longer as sluggish as you need to. Group leaders have a hard and fast itinerary to stick to and should get you to base camp and lower back with the aid of using a precise date. In exercise what this indicates is you may forestall for breaks after they advise and hit the trek once more after they advise. (It isn't unknown for companies to bypass acclimatisation days, setting customers at dangers in an effort to meet their deadlines. This is typically due to the fact they may be looking to play capture-up after a not on time flight into Lukla). You will of route have a sure quantity of freedom – as you're all going the identical manner you could continually capture up later. But that is a negative replacement for the real freedom of creating your very own selections and being at no one's beckon name. A really releasing feeling that need to be skilled as a minimum as soon as in a lifetime.

- A stronger feeling of self-worth. No feelings of inadequacy making you feel even worse if you can't keep up with the rest of the group or your guide/porter combo. When Janet and I went on the Lares trail with our wonderful guide, Maritza, she was extremely considerate. It was clear we hadn't trekked before and neither of us were very fit. She didn't hurry us along. On the contrary she kept telling us to take it slow. Did that make us feel any better? Not a bit. The fact is she was always twenty or thirty yards ahead of us and we couldn't keep up. Being a human being, you can't help but feel hurried under those circumstances. And it wouldn't have mattered if she'd been twenty yards behind instead – due to the fact Maritza become simplest preventing due to the fact we stopped. Like it or now no longer, Maritza's presence however stress on us, regardless of all her efforts now no longer to. On EBC trek I frequently imagined it'd be a nightmare to be in that identical position.

- Meeting new people. You are never alone when you trek solo. There's an argument to be made that you will meet more people this way than you ever would in a group. Groups can be very insular, where everyone tends to mix with each other and few people outside the group. When you go it alone you are stopping and talking to new people all the time. Some you will meet once and by no means see once more (they're frequently going the other direction). Others you may meet constantly alongside the manner. They becomes part of your Base Camp enjoy and also you part of theirs.

- Bragging rights. There's just no getting away from it, solo trekking to Everest Base Camp gives you stronger bragging rights even if the only person you ever tell is yourself. You'll know you've achieved something worthwhile, because it didn't come easy. You spent months preparing before setting out and then you hit the trail. And it hurt, sometime a lot. But you made it, with no-one to push you or encourage you. You made it all by yourself.

- One that may only apply to a tiny minority of people but is worth mentioning. If, like me, you plan on someday going on a wilderness trek like the Pacific Crest Trail, this is a good step in that direction. Rather than step straight into wilderness trekking it is a good idea to first discover if you're going to like being alone for prolonged periods. It's not for everyone. At the very least it would be wise to know if you're comfortable with carrying a rucksack on your back for hours while putting one foot in front of the other.

Solo trekking doesn't mean having to be alone. (That's me on the right)

LANGUAGE

English is extensively spoken in Nepal, so that you could have few issues communicating. The generally used greeting is 'Namaste', which you'll locate your self announcing a lot. Other trekkers use it to greet every different in addition to Nepalese – aleven though I couldn't assist noticing that the better you get and the thinner the air becomes, many inn to simply announcing 'Hi' due to the fact it's easier.

FOOD

The golden rule whilst journeying to any us of a is to devour nearby dishes. That can also additionally appear apparent to a few, however I'm from the UK - in which many an person has long gone overseas and been bowled over and saddened to find out the English breakfast they ordered isn't the identical culinary satisfaction as the only from their nearby greasy spoon. Food in Nepal is some thing in itself to appearance ahead to. A trekker's favorite are Momos – dumplings, fried or steamed, which come full of beef, chook or vegetables. They are yummy, quick, reasonably-priced and filling. I venture you now no longer to like them.

The countrywide dish is Dal Bhat – extra a meeting of dishes than one unmarried dish. It is composed particularly of, lentils (dal) and rice (bhat) and an collection of vegetable aspect dishes the use of quite a few spices. It varies an excessive amount of to be any extra specific, however it's tough to move incorrect with this dish anyplace you move.

Sherpa Stew – to be had everywhere, tasty and nutritious, containing because it does, a aggregate of vegetables, beans and noodles.

For breakfast Western palates are properly catered for. Choose from pancakes, muesli, eggs and toast, jam, honey, porridge etc.

Yak Steaks. I spoke to a person who attempted the sort of in Pheriche and defined it as having the feel of rubber, at the same time as now no longer almost as tasty. By contrast, I ordered one on the Khumbu Lodge in Namche and it become the first-class steak I've ever had in my life. I'm a touch ashamed to confess that, as I'm what you would possibly name an uncommitted vegetarian. By uncommitted I suggest I strive my first-class now no longer to devour meat (for moral reasons) and approximately ninety-5 in keeping with cent of the time I succeed. But now and again I'm faced with the choice of a juicy burger or on this example yak steak, and I succumb to temptation. The simplest upside I can think about to being an uncommitted vegetarian is that I can by no means get too excessive and effective approximately folks that devour meat. The disadvantage is on every occasion I do I go through a touch little bit of shame. I then promise myself I will move even longer subsequent time earlier than ingesting meat once more. Let's face it, being vegetarian is tough and I don't have anything however admiration for folks that control it with overall consistency. But in a few approaches being an uncommitted vegetarian is even harder, specially whilst ingesting out. As a non-cook, pretty much the whole lot I can conjure up myself is quite bland besides and being vegetarian doesn't make an entire lot of difference.

But on the ones uncommon events I devour out I sense I deserve a destroy from the blandness. So as a praise for my half-hearted vegetarian efforts I'll frequently deal with myself to that burger! Then hate myself afterwards. The worst is whilst you are offered together along with your alternatives in advance, like whilst requested when you have any unique nutritional necessities earlier than going somewhere. Because that includes creating a dedication from which there may be typically no turning returned. You can't inform your host you're a vegetarian then extrade your thoughts later and inform them you're now no longer after all! How embarrassing could that be?

On arrival in Peru, Janet, an similarly uncommitted vegetarian, and I have been met with the aid of using a host-manual to take us to our hotel, and deliver us with our

itinerary, along with the Lares trail - in which we'd be taking meals to prepare dinner dinner at the trek. Sitting in the front seat of the car he turned and asked us the fateful question; "Do you have any special dietary requirements? I hesitated before taking the plunge and making a commitment from which there would be no getting out of once on the trail.

"We're each vegetarian", I

stated. "Do you devour fish?"

he enquired. "Yes", I replied.

Then a pause.

"And chicken", stated Janet.

(Somewhere a vegetarian rolls their eyes).

As some distance because the yak steak goes - yaks are stunning animals and the yak steak on the Khumbu Lodge haunts me a touch even now. Apparently plenty of what passes for yak steak withinside the Khumbu is truely buffalo steak. Not that it makes a difference – an animal is an animal. For what it's worth, it turned into the simplest time I ate meat at the same time as in Nepal. It's a rustic in which it in reality is straightforward to be a vegetarian.

As nicely as an abundance of teahouses there are various tiny stores at the trek in which you could purchase snacks to preserve you going.

One of many shops along the trek. This one has a fierce guard dog to deter shoplifters.

MONEY

In October 2015 a hundred rupees equalled precisely one US dollar, which makes intellectual mathematics extraordinarily clean in case you're from the US. You can't purchase rupees outdoor of Nepal and it's unlawful to take them out apparently, so you'll must wait till you get there. It's essential you are taking sufficient cash with you to closing at some stage in the trek, as there aren't anyt any ATMs above Namche.

A large plus is all rupees are in be aware form – because of this that now no longer having to hold masses of cash round. Denominations are 5, 10, 20, 50, a hundred, 500 and a thousand rupees.

From what I ought to see all forex exchanges provide precisely the equal price in Thamel, so there's little factor in buying round. As with all forex exchanges, they may provide you with a majority of the very best price notes, so make a factor of inquiring for smaller denominations (100s are pleasant) as converting larger notes may be hard at the trek. You ought to be satisfactory with 500s – it's the a thousand rupee notes you ought to avoid.

Don't neglect about to allow your financial institution recognize you're going to Nepal so you don't revel in any issues whilst chickening out cash from ATMs. It's also an idea to put essential bank telephone numbers (including country code) in your cell phone contacts list before you leave so if you do run into difficulties you can quickly call them instead of having to search for the number.

CRIME

Nepal is one of the most secure locations withinside the world. Violent crime is sort of unprecedented even in Kathmandu, and you could stroll round at any time of the day or night time with out feeling threatened. As in maximum cities, you ought to be aware about pickpockets and convey your pockets/handbag inner your coat. Guys - if you really have no choice but to carry your wallet in your back pocket (it's very hot and you're going out in just a t-shirt and not carrying a bag) then here's a tip I saw from the world's best pickpocket (turned upright citizen) on a simple method to prevent pickpockets stealing it - put your wallet in your back pocket horizontally instead of vertically. We all certainly region it vertically due to the fact it's less complicated to get it out. Insert it horizontally as an alternative, with the hole face down and you'll have problem getting it out yourself. Alternatively, check those outstanding pickpocket evidence tour garments on those sites:

A suitable concept earlier than visiting everywhere is to open a financial savings account with the equal financial institution in which you maintain your essential account. Keep the majority of your cash on this and right away switch cash throughout on line as and whilst needed. That way, if the worst occurs and your financial institution card is stolen, the thieves will simplest be capable of get entry to the small quantity on your essential account and now no longer completely smooth you out.

As a Westerner you'll be approached through human beings in Kathmandu (specially Thamel), seeking to promote you pills and a myriad of frequently indecipherable items. These are extra of a nuisance than something and there's no want to experience threatened. You buy their wares at your very own risk, of course.

Beggars

Like any major city, Kathmandu has its share of beggars. One thing I read constantly before leaving was of the number of children begging in Thamel. I don't know what happened to them but in October 2015 I saw none at all.

There were, of course, plenty of adult beggars. I get a little irked when every travel blog I come across strongly advises never to give to beggars, the reason being it makes them 'dependant on tourists'. By this logic - scaling things up a little - we shouldn't give foreign aid to third world countries either. Is there a difference? Not that I can see. Other than when giving to individuals you can be fairly certain the money is reaching the people for whom it was intended.

I suspect the same people who advocate not giving to beggars in third world countries would tell you not to give to beggars at home either, because: "They'll only spend it on alcohol and drugs", ignoring the fact that a good percentage of the working population chooses to do the same. Beggars may well spend some of the money they acquire this way, but they also have to eat. If it bothers you, buy them some food instead.

It is tough now no longer to be touched through the plight of folks that are infinitely poorer than yourself. One hundred rupees right here or there isn't going to extrade anyone's existence however it simply would possibly purchase them their subsequent meal. An antique Nepalese guy started crying after I exceeded him six hundred rupees in Kathmandu. Anyone might have idea I'd given him one million dollars. Six hundred rupees is six dollars – the price of a espresso in a few locations withinside the West. And not anything in comparison to the cash I've spent on crap over the years. Do I suppose this makes me a great person? Not really. Giving cash you may effortlessly have the funds for is, nicely... easy. And I've been at the receiving give up of kindness a long way extra frequently. Here's a real story:

I become 16 and had hitch-hiked from my fatherland of Belfast to Dublin's truthful metropolis to enlist on one of these drug trials wherein they pay you masses of cash for being a human guinea pig. I hadn't counted on now no longer getting admitted on certainly considered one among the pains and having to hitch-hike domestic prematurely, with out a penny in my pocket.

After an afternoon seeking to hitch-hike out of Dublin I had spectacularly did not placed any profitable distance among myself and the metropolis. I had walked all day and gotten one ride - from a man in a tractor who took me 1 / 4 mile

in addition alongside the road (at on foot speed), earlier than turning off closer to his farm.

A couple of nights formerly I had slept out in a park and frozen 1/2 of to dying in my reasonably-priced artificial napping bag that become no higher than a skinny sheet. So as nightfall fell I realised I become dealing with some other dreaded sleepless night time withinside the open. Tired, hungry and getting chillier through the minute, I knew I needed to consider some thing fast. I reached a tiny bridge above a fast-flowing flow and hurled my napping bag into it, a good way to pressure myself to take a few drastic action. Without a plan, I headed lower back closer to a bit metropolis known as Swords, which I'd walked thru earlier.

Once on the town I requested men if they may spare a cigarette. One of the guys gave me 3 cigarettes and, with out my asking, cash for a cup of tea. I ought to have gave the look of I may want to use one.

Instead of purchasing a cup of tea I used the cash to hop on a bus returned into Dublin. I made my manner to O'Connell Street railway station, wherein I was hoping I ought to someway get on a teach or as a minimum spend the night time in relative warmth. I hung across the station because the 8 o'clock teach to Belfast pulled into platform one. There turned into a defend at the gate checking tickets, but none on platform, wherein no trains have been due. The station itself turned into crawling with guards, however. So I waited for the proper second – once they could all concurrently appearance the opposite manner and I ought to slip thru the gate to platform and get throughout the tracks. The second by no means came. And so at one minute to 8 I ought to wait no longer. I driven open the gate and walked thru. What I didn't recognise turned into a group of guards have been sat gambling playing cards at the back of a small hut on the opposite side. "Hello", I said, with all of the self assurance I ought to muster, and carried on walking, seeking to seem like I had each proper to be there. Further up the platform there has been a timber bridge and I didn't want to go the tracks. I ran throughout the bridge as rapid as my legs could convey me and down the opposite side, leaping at the teach simply because it turned into taking off. Then sat in a bathroom for the -hour journey, protecting the door ajar so the price price tag inspector could assume it turned into empty. An hour after that I turned into home.

I cite this right here to demonstrate how a bit kindness can cross a protracted manner – perhaps in methods you can by no means anticipate. Ultimately giving to beggars ought to be your very own choice – and now no longer primarily based totally on the advice of a few blogger who's too tight to position their hand of their pocket and now no longer sincere sufficient to name it what it is.

Scammers

There is one little rip-off you ought to be conscious of, which I skilled first hand. Opportunists will method you and ask you to shop for them milk (or food) for his or her child. When you provide them cash (let's say two hundred rupees) they may gallantly decline. They will ask you to as a substitute accompany them to the grocery store (commonly some yards away) and purchase the products for them. When you get to the grocery store you'll find out why they weren't eager to simply accept a miserly two hundred rupees for the reason that powdered milk prices 900 rupees! And that's only for starters – a few have a small purchasing list. If you're idiot sufficient to component together along with your cash, a quick time later they may go back to the grocery store and get their (your) cash returned at the items, which they're unfastened to spend but they like (probable on alcohol and drugs).

STAYING CONNECTED

Avoid roaming costs through shopping for a Nepalese sim card at one in all dozens of retailers in Thamel, or everywhere in Kathmandu (besides the airport wherein, like the whole thing else, it's extra expensive). Look for telecellsmartphone stores with the NCELL logo. Another issuer is Nepal Telecom. Opinions are divided as to which of those is the best. You'll want your passport and a passport photo (and an unlocked telecellsmartphone on the way to use it). The seller will photocopy your passport, insert the sim and cargo it together along with your preferred credit. If your telecellsmartphone calls for a micro sim they may reduce the sim to length and insert it so it works.

For the ones with out cellular net get entry to on their gadgets many teahouses provide unfastened Wi-Fi, however don't be amazed whilst you attempt to join and the proprietor tells you it's now no longer running on the second. After some time you can't assist however assume it's only a ruse to get you thru the door. If so, you need to recognize their ingenuity, given how a whole lot opposition they face. Other teahouses provide Wi-Fi at a cost. They deliver little playing cards – both 250 rupees or a thousand rupees, with a password that you'll want a magnifying glass to read. These allegedly ultimate for twenty-four hours. A inn proprietor attempted to persuade me that it's now no longer 24 hours from whilst you begin the usage of it however 24 hours overall use – however I critically doubt it. These are certainly now no longer true value, specially if there's a strength outage or the net is going down.

Prepaid Wifi cards - when all else fails.

POWERING YOUR DEVICES

I added a sun charger with me and I advise you do too. Few resorts have strength sockets withinside the rooms so you'll must pay to price your tool withinside the not unusualplace room. Unless there's a strength strip to be had you could want to attend till a person else's telecellsmartphone finishes charging first. See GEAR bankruptcy for similarly info.

TRAVEL INSURANCE

Don't pass with out doing away with journey coverage – clean and simple. While it can experience like spending a whole lot of cash for some thing you may't maintain for your hand, if some thing is going incorrect it'll appear to be small alternate in comparison to what it'll value to get you off the trek and perhaps pay for health center treatment. Insurance is one of these demanding matters in existence you don't truly respect till you want it. Make certain you get the precise stage of coverage too – popular journey coverage won't reduce it. Make certain the quilt you pick now no longer simplest covers hiking (can also additionally come under 'Adventure activities'), however additionally the

suitable altitude (over 5000 metres). Read the important points and make sure it consists of emergency helicopter evacuation. I used the British Mountaineering Council (BMC). I've additionally heard top reviews approximately World Nomads.

Vaccinations

Vaccinations aren't required to go into Nepal however are noticeably advisable, nonetheless – in as a whole lot as there's a totally actual threat you can come to remorse it in case you don't get them. Some require a direction, which could take numerous weeks - so make sure you permit your self sufficient time to start the direction earlier than your trip.

Diptheria – infection from breathing droplets unfold aleven though human contact

Hepatitis A – infected meals or water

Tetanus – infection of cuts and burns with tetanus spores located in soil

Typhoid - infected meals or water

Cholera - infected meals or water

Hepatitis B – infected needles, sexual contact, blood products

Japanese Encephalitis – bites from inflamed mosquitos

Rabies – bites from dogs, rats and different inflamed animals

Visas

You can reap your visa out of your neighborhood Nepalese Embassy earlier than you leave, both in individual or via way of means of post. Alternatively you may purchase one on arrival at Tribhuvan International Airport in Kathmandu. A examine the Nepalese Embassy internet site can also additionally convince you choosing one up on arrival is the easiest, maximum truthful option. If you're from one of the following nations unluckily you haven't any desire however to use earlier than going:

- Nigeria
- Ghana
-

Zimbabwe

Swaziland

Cameroon

Somalia

Liberia

Ethiopia

Iraq

Palestine

Afghanistan

Syria

There are 3 kinds of vacationer visas.

15 days = $25

30 days = $40

ninety days = $100

You will want the 30 day visa. If acquiring on the airport, make certain you deliver passport photos (It's now no longer a catastrophe in case you don't – there's a man with a digital digicam who will take a few for you). Note – whilst they are saying greenbacks they suggest greenbacks. You can't pay on your visa in some other currency.

Permits

As a solo-trekker you'll want kinds of documentation earlier than setting out your EBC trek:

Free Individual Trekkers (FIT) Permit - This is a widespread permit, which have to be received earlier than hiking everywhere in Nepal. Despite the call it isn't loose (it as soon as was). Free on this context manner you're loose to move alone. The price is presently 2000 NR and may be received from the places of work of the Nepal Tourist Board (or Tourism Service Centre) in Bhrikuti Mandap,

Those journeying with a set are required to get a Trekker Information Management System (TIMS) permit – aleven though it must be covered as a part of your package.

As nicely as elevating sales for Nepal the lets in permit the authorities to preserve tabs on what number of trekkers go to the region every yr in addition to offer a tough concept wherein you're in case you get lost.

Sagamartha National Park Entrance Permit. This also can be received on the Tourism Service Centre or even as at the trek itself - on the checkpoint simply beyond the village of Monjo. Fee: 3000 NR plus VAT

ALTITUDE SICKNESS

It can strike every body from a amateur trekker to the maximum skilled mountaineer. It's crucial to recognize that there may be no regarded correlation among altitude illness and health levels. That said, a few humans are greater prone than others and there's no actual manner of understanding that you are. At altitude the air stress receives fairly thinner the better you pass, which means there may be much less oxygen in each breath you take. This makes you war for breath that allows you to get greater oxygen into your lungs. The frame responds via way of means of developing greater crimson blood cells that allows you to bring the oxygen around. In impact this creates a thickening of the blood.

The great manner to AVOID altitude illness is to ascend slowly, and diligently adhere to the ones acclimatisation days. Experts suggest to 'stroll high, sleep low' which means you must sleep decrease than the very best altitude you attain every day.

This isn't usually possible, of route. More sensible recommendation is to now no longer ascend greater than one thousand meters each day and now no longer sleep better than three hundred meters than the night time before. And drink plenty of fluids! If you suspect you've got got altitude illness the first-class route of movement is to descend immediately. Altitude illness can kill.

My simplest preceding revel in of altitude illness became in Peru, whilst at an altitude of 4000 meters I felt like my head would possibly explode. The simplest different factor I skilled became lack of appetite, however that is pretty not unusualplace at altitude and might not be taken as a signal of some thing serious. There are sorts of pretty excessive altitude illness and also you need to be aware about the symptoms:

HAPE – High-altitude pulmonary edema

This is the maximum not unusualplace of the 2 and may strike at altitudes above 2500 meters. HAPE is due to the lungs swelling with fluid.

- Difficulty breathing even while resting
- Coughing
- Tightness in the chest
- Decreased performance levels
- Rapid heart rate
- Blue skin colour

HACE – High-altitude cerebral edema

HACE is much less not unusualplace, and is much more likely to strike above 4000 meters. HACE is due to the mind swelling with fluid.

- Severe headaches
- Confusion/disorientation
- Lethargy
- Nausea
- Loss of consciousness

DIAMOX

You can use Diamox as both prevention towards or a treatment for altitude illness. Prior to leaving for Base Camp I went to a consultant journey medical doctor who recommended me to start taking it the instant I arrived in

Kathmandu, 1/2 of a pill withinside the morning, 1/2 of withinside the afternoon. This got here as some thing of a wonder due to the fact till then I had simplest study/heard of humans taking it AFTER they have been struck down with altitude illness – with blended results.

How I study it this: it's a as soon as in an entire life trip. Do I need to run the chance of now no longer making it to Base Camp due to altitude illness, after having spent months preparing, money on a flight and travelled half way across the world? Am I going to take my chances and hope if I do get altitude sickness the Diamox will alleviate it when I'm there? Or am I going to cut down the risks enormously by taking the travel doctor's advice?

Earthquake damage

In April 2015 Nepal became struck through a devastating importance 7.eight earthquake, accompanied 17 days later through every other, measuring 7.3. Many villages have been absolutely destroyed and over 9000 humans misplaced their lives, together with 19 humans buried through an avalanche at Base Camp (10 of them Sherpas). While now no longer absolutely unscathed, the earthquake did now no longer have an effect on the Khumbu place pretty as badly as many different components of Nepal. Some homes have been destroyed (and are presently being rebuilt) however the path itself has been cleared. Tourism has been hit badly – I actually have study reviews that vacationer numbers are down as a whole lot as 85%. I discover it unfathomable that humans might live farfar from a rustic in such numbers due to some thing that's already happened. There isn't anyt any greater or much less hazard of every other earthquake this 12 months than there's in say, 5 years, or ten. Such is the character of earthquakes. In any case, Nepal's misfortune approach there's no higher time to move than proper now. One difficulty I had approximately getting into October became that I might have problem locating an area to live. I had study many bills of teahouses filling up fast at some point of this month. This became now no longer the case in 2015, six months after the earthquake struck. In one resort I became the simplest guest.

Trail repair is underway.

FUEL CRISIS

As if Nepal didn't have sufficient troubles, in September 2015 the Indian authorities halted overland trade, growing a gas shortage (Nepal imports all of its petroleum from India). Suddenly each taxi driving force became doubling their costs and blaming the gas crisis. In February 2016 the embargo became lifted. However, I suspect that now taxi drivers recognise how a whole lot Westerners are inclined to pay to get round they'll be reluctant to move lower back to the vintage costs (and who can blame them). Even in the event that they don't, fares are nevertheless very affordable and now no longer some thing to fear approximately unduly.

On a wall in Thamel - one person's response to the embargo

GENERAL GEAR ADVICE

The sheer quantity of desire to be had could make the system of purchasing the proper equipment sense overwhelming. But it is able to additionally be a variety of amusing or even addictive if you're now no longer careful. The major mistake humans make, specially whilst hiking for the primary time, is bringing an excessive amount of stuff, a whole lot of that is unnecessary. So in addition to taking simplest the ones belongings you truely can't do with out there are 3 issues whilst shopping for equipment:

- Weight
- Cost
- Quality/durability

As you'll be wearing the whole thing in your lower back weight is manifestly a chief element in deciding on what to buy. You need to goal at a most weight of 10kg. However I might emphasise that no unmarried element need to dominate the opposite. Here's why:

Most producers of backpacking equipment attempt to make their merchandise as

light-weight as feasible nowadays and are constantly growing new substances or strategies to outdo remaining year's model. While that is honestly a terrific thing, a number of those are prohibitively and questionably luxurious. By 'questionably' I suggest I actually have critical doubts that the modern day ultra-light-weight water-resistant outer layer is really well worth the $four hundred asking charge. This is borne out with the aid of using the critiques provided with the aid of using many web sites who take a look at stated objects for a full-size duration of time. The antique saying 'You get what you pay for' can most effective be taken so far. I suspect what dictates the charge of many objects has much less to do with first-class than it has to do with branding and the restricted amount produced. By the identical token it's miles tremendously not likely a $30 dozing bag goes to be as excessive first-class as a $250 one. Buying tools consequently is some thing of a balancing act, which calls for you operate your judgement and determine wherein your priorities lie.

If Everest Base Camp Trek is possibly to be the most effective trek you ever intend to do then first-class/sturdiness won't be as tons of an problem than in case you wish to apply it into the future. I desired to shop for tools that became now no longer most effective mild however might remaining for decades to come, so became organized a bit greater - at the same time as maintaining it real. Below is a listing of the objects I took to Base Camp (and a pair I didn't), accompanied with the aid of using an in-intensity examine every object anywhere feasible. Let me simply say that I haven't any association with any of the manufacturers right here and am now no longer receiving a fee for whatever I recommend (I need to be so lucky). If I rave approximately a specific product it's due to the fact I became honestly overjoyed with the way it performed. The reality is I became glad with each object I took – the praise for having spent a lot time getting to know every in turn. There are some of first-rate web sites you need to use that will help you determine which tools to shop for. The one I used maximum became   These men take a look at pretty much the whole lot to inside an inch of its life.

Finally - you could purchase each little bit of trekking tools beneathneath the solar in Thamel, the big majority of it inferior first-class rip-offs of famous manufacturers at a fragment of the cost. Tempting as it can be, it's first-class to keep away from inexpensive first-class objects that could disintegrate at some point of your trek or sincerely now no longer characteristic as they're intended. Whatever you do, don't purchase boots. There also are some stores promoting real call manufacturers. Don't count on to make any financial savings right here. A few objects I noticed have been extra luxurious than shopping for at home. Think of Thamel because the area to shop for much less vital objects or belongings you forgot to %. You also can lease tools on your trek inexpensively, in case you don't see your self the usage of it regularly sufficient to justify a big outlay. Something else to endure in thoughts when

packing is many teahouses provide reasonably-priced laundry facilities, which means you could get your garments washed in preference to packing that greater t-blouse and socks.

GEAR LIST

The following consists of what you'll be carrying while you get at the plane. Therefore three x pairs of socks consists of those you've got got on.

- Rucksack
- Sleeping bag
- Trekking poles + pole tips
- Stuff sack
- Pillow case
- Sunglasses x 2 with hard case
- Boots
- Sandals or flip-flops
- Smartwool socks x 3
- Gloves
- Base Layers
- Mid layers
- Down jacket
- Hiking trousers x 2
- Hat
- Buff
- Toilet Roll
- Travel towel
- Water Purification system.
- Water bottle
- Money belt/pouch
- Map
- Camera
- E-Reader
- Solar charger
- Travel adapter
- Head-torch
-

Sun cream
- Chapstick
- First Aid Kit
- Pocket ashtray
- Earplugs

Rucksack

The remaining time I wore a rucksack for any full-size period of time became hitch-trekking round France on the smooth age of sixteen. I will in no way neglect about how uncomfortable it became. Right from the off the straps reduce into my shoulders, inflicting me to shift the load from one shoulder to the alternative each few minutes. It became an agonizing revel in and one I became now no longer hectic to repeat. Thankfully rucksack layout has moved on a bit on account That then. That, mixed with the understanding of the way first-class to % a rucksack (see later chapter), supposed I didn't have to. There are varieties of rucksack to consider – inner body and outside body. The latter are going out of style and carrying one can also additionally make you appear to be you stepped out of a time machine. Most human beings are choosing inner body nowadays as they're sincerely extra snug and higher designed.

While weight is a top attention it shouldn't be the handiest one. You don't need to pick a light-weight rucksack if it's going to crumble on the seams at the same time as you're at the trek. I offered a Black Diamond Mercury sixty five for its many first rate features. It weighed in at 4lb empty, that's a long way too heavy for a few hikers' tastes. But it didn't feel heavy once it was on my back and by the end of my trek I'd fallen in love with it and didn't want to take it off! If buying from a shop you should try it on before buying – ask the nice assistant for advice. People who paintings in equipment stores are typically skilled backpackers or climbers and realize what they're speakme approximately. If shopping for on-line ensure to shop for in advance of time in case you need to go back it – load it up, move for a protracted stroll and notice the way it feels. Your hips ought to take maximum of the weight, now no longer your shoulders. Make positive you fasten up all of the straps in place of simply permit them to dangle– it makes a significant consolation difference.

One different attention while selecting is to shop for one that gives get entry to from the front. Some rucksacks are purely 'top-loaders', which means you may handiest get your equipment inside and out from the huge beginning on the top. This is a actual ache while the component you need is at the lowest of your rucksack and also you have

to tug the whole lot else out to attain it.

Sleeping bag

This is one of these objects wherein there may be a long way an excessive amount of choice. Cut your alternatives in 1/2 of with the aid of using selecting a down slumbering bag over a artificial one. The latter are tons heavier and don't % away almost as well. The handiest ahem… drawback to a down slumbering bag (and it hardly ever subjects on a teahouse trek) is that they can take a long term to dry in the event that they get wet. Keep it in a drybag and it gained't. Narrow your picks similarly nonetheless with the aid of using going for a 3-4-season bag. It can get very bloodless at night time any time of yr withinside the Khumbu region, even at the same time as wrapped up in mattress in a teahouse. Check the temperature score earlier than shopping for.

Reading critiques for slumbering baggage you'll discover that hikers can get a touch anal at times. It appears that no slumbering bag on this planet is exempt from vilification with the aid of using a few expert, (who appears to have owned an inordinate range of slumbering baggage for one lifetime), locating fault with the smallest component. Try now no longer to allow this be off putting – maximum of the baggage they generally tend to check might be great for EBC trekking. Some dependable manufacturers are Marmot, Western Mountaineering, Feathered Friends.

I become first of all drawn to a German synthetic bag known as Yeti Passion Five, that's marketed because the lightest slumbering bag withinside the international and has gained numerous awards. This added me to the Yeti range. In the stop I went for the Yeti VIB six hundred as I had doubts approximately the Passion Five being heat enough. The VIB six hundred has an high temperature score of -23 (which made me sense safe), weighing in at a first rate 1.040g. It got here with an impossibly small stuff sack, which, besides for the reality it become furnished with the bag, you would possibly suppose it become intended for some thing else - like sporting your toothbrush. After a protracted battle I sooner or later controlled it, however determined I definitely didn't need a combat on my arms each morning while it got here to packing it away. I left it at domestic and purchased a far extra accommodating stuff sack, which additionally had the gain of being waterproof.

Stuff sack

Using a stuff sack lets you compress your equipment right into a smaller area the use of a chain of straps related at each ends through a floating lid that suits tightly over

the cinched stop (see picture). I offered two - one for my slumbering bag and one for my garments so I wouldn't always have to tug out every to get to the different. This stored my equipment organised with the introduced consolation of understanding it become included if my rucksack fell withinside the river or I met with a torrential downpour. I selected the Sea to Summit eVENT Compression Dry Sack primarily based totally on overwhelmingly effective critiques. Make positive you select out the proper length earlier than shopping for.

Trekking Poles

Some hard-center backpackers suppose those are a piece of a con. I wasn't a fan myself earlier than EBC, having determined them pretty tough to get the dangle of in Peru and on an afternoon trek up Snowdon just a few months earlier. I considered

now no longer bringing a couple in any respect then discovered myself the sufferer of an impulse purchase even as surfing a tenting save in Brighton (with all of the lack of confidence of now no longer having examine at the least 10 evaluations first). I then needed to hurry domestic and test the evaluations to make certain I hadn't made a mistake! As success might have it, the Black Diamond poles had been a pretty rated set of poles and some thing I may have ended up shopping for anyway. For sensible functions hiking poles are very beneficial while going uphill as they provide you with greater leverage to drag your self up. When happening they lend greater assist to forestall you from slipping in addition to taking plenty of the pressure off your knees. Most poles are adjustable, permitting you to shorten them for going uphill (keep away from leaning back) and prolong while happening (keep away from leaning over). Make certain to examine the instructions - maximum humans generally tend to position their fingers thru the pinnacle of the straps, inflicting the straps to simply cling across the wrist, serving no motive in any respect. The accurate manner is to position your fingers thru from underneath. This transfers the strain out of your fingers onto your wrists and lets in for a far extra steady grip.

Trekking pole tip protectors

I'm surprised hiking poles don't include those included. You won't discover them on maximum tools web sites either. You are going to want to percent your hiking poles interior your rucksack earlier than getting on a plane (you could't carry them as keep on luggage) to save you them from getting broken or stolen. There's a completely actual danger the pointy recommendations will punch a hollow thru the canvas as soon as the luggage handlers begin throwing it around. Avoid this eventuality with a couple of reasonably-priced pole tip protectors from Amazon or eBay. Quite other than that the rubber recommendations offer a higher grip on rocky surfaces wherein metallic ones can frequently slide.

Pillowcase

Putting it bluntly, a number of the pillows furnished withinside the resorts aren't as smooth as they may be. Bringing your very own pillowcase to position on them may appear to be overkill however you'll be happy you did.

A pillowcase could be very light-weight and may be folded effortlessly and tucked away to your slumbering bag. An opportunity to the use of a pillow in any respect is to fill your stuff-sack with clothes, wrap it in a heat fleece, and use that instead.

Sunglasses x2 with hard case

Sunglasses are an vital item. Bring a spare pair and preserve them in a difficult case to save you damage. Yes, you could purchase sun shades in Nepal, however it's sod's regulation that in case you destroy or lose them while you'll be nowhere close to everywhere you could select out up a couple. Must defend in opposition to UV rays, aleven though definitely they all do those days.

Boots

Undoubtedly the maximum crucial piece of package you'll purchase, as you won't get a ways in uncomfortable or insufficient footwear. I already owned a couple of heavy leather-based taking walks boots, which I changed into going to use, now no longer wondering weight might be a difficulty as I might be carrying them. Then I realised lifting my toes may end up an problem after some time and it changed into simply as crucial what I changed into carrying on them be mild too. I desired to make matters as clean for myself as I probably could. So I offered a brand new pair of Merrell's, which had been considerably lighter, extraordinarily snug and waterproof.

Whatever boots you purchase, make certain they offer exact ankle assist and put on them in earlier than you leave. That said, the Merrels didn't require any carrying in, they had been snug from the primary time I positioned them on. Great boots deserving in their reputation.

Sandals or flip-flops

After a difficult day's hiking you could sense like taking your boots off and enjoyable into some thing extra snug for wandering across the village or chilling withinside the lodge. Many humans carry a couple of sandals or flip-flops as they're mild to hold and don't absorb plenty space. I didn't bother, as I'm now no longer genuinely a sandals or flip-flops carrying form of guy .

Smartwool socks

I genuinely hate having bloodless toes and desired to keep away from this in any respect costs. When I first got here throughout Smartwool socks I changed into greatly surprised through the price (as a person who's used to shopping for three pairs of socks for a fiver). However the unanimous superb evaluations on those made me take the plunge. It changed into an advantage to examine

And finally find out they don't scent even if you've been sporting them for a week - which saves having to carry too many pairs as you won't want to exalternate them almost as frequently as ordinary socks. Before going I examine some of testimonies of trekkers getting blisters on EBC. I haven't any manner of understanding whether or not it changed into the boots or the socks I chose, or a aggregate of each, however I didn't even come near getting a blister or having any hassle with my feet. Another emblem with a exceptional reputation, aleven though I've but to strive them, are Darn Tough socks.

Gloves

It's now no longer essential to spend massive on these. Ski gloves are too cumbersome and a piece over the top. Just a heat pair of gloves or mittens have to suffice. Many human beings select the latter as they permit your palms to live collectively and thereby percentage frame warmness. The exchange off is you lose the dexterity you get with gloves. For Base Camp hiking I assume gloves are preferable.

Base Layers

Base layers are worn subsequent to the pores and skin so have to have right wicking features to soak up sweat. Once you prevent moving, sweat quick cools, inflicting you to get very cold very quick. While a few base layers may be a bit expensive they may be really well worth spending out on in preference to making do with a hard and fast of thermals out of your nearby supermarket.

Merino

Merino wool is really well worth shopping for for the distinction in weight alone. It's smooth at the pores and skin, consequently feels hotter, and is in particular right at soaking up odours which means you could break out with sporting it for longer and likely make do with one set on quick journey like EBC. Brands to do not forget are Icebreaker and Patagonia. A tons extra pricey desire than it's artificial cousin, it have to be noted.

Synthetic

Synthetic base layers are relatively reasonably-priced if you're on a price range and a few provide pretty right wicking features. The disadvantage is that they can get pretty pungent very quick. A emblem I didn't find out till coming back from Everest, however
comes exceptionally recommended, is Helly Hansen. Other manufacturers really well worth a glance are
Berghaus and North Face.

Mid-layers

Layering – When figuring out what garments to carry, you'll live hotter with the aid of using sporting some of thinner layers than one thick layer. This is due to the fact trapped air maintains warmness subsequent for your frame. The introduced gain is you could get rid of and upload layers as wished both to calm down or heat up. A right fleece in aggregate with lengthy sleeve t-shirts will suffice. Avoid whatever cotton as it's far gradual to dry if it receives wet. I offered a Rab Power Stretch Pull- on Beluga after analyzing a evaluate from an skilled backpacker who swore with the aid of using his. Something approximately it simply fills you with self belief while going through the elements.

Down jacket

This is what you'll see maximum different trekkers sporting. A seven-hundred or 800 down fill is recommended. The opposition in mild-weight down jackets has taken off nowadays and a few are very pricey, so it's really well worth buying around. I used a reasonably-priced non-branded one from a UK save referred to as Decathalon, which befell to have massive interior pockets (uncommon in a down jacket), with a Berghaus gilet underneath.

Rain/Windproof jacket

Glad I introduced mine. Even aleven though it didn't rain on my trek there have been instances while the wind could have reduce thru my down jacket and gilet combo, making for a few very bloodless hiking. Some of the high-quit range weigh subsequent to not anything and fee a small fortune. The very truth they weigh so little makes me even extra reluctant to element with the coins and undermines my religion in a number of the claims with the aid of using their makers. I'm now no longer going to mention tons extra. Instead

I'll permit climber Andy Kirkpatrick do the talking. This is a hyperlink to his insightful article: 'The Truth About Waterproof Breathable Fabrics'. (For what it's really well worth my very own fee approximately $50 from Mountain Warehouse and changed into simply fine).

Hiking trousers

The key attention is shopping some thing each mild and quick-drying. Don't even reflect onconsideration on sporting jeans – denim is heavy, bulky and extraordinarily gradual to dry if it receives wet. I opted for two pairs of Fjallraven Nils Trousers, which appear like ordinary trousers, (in place of the trekking pants look). These have been very mild, at the same time as nonetheless being rugged. They're pretty pricey for trekking trousers however, as with maximum of my gear, I invested for the lengthy term.

Hat

A heat woolly hat is essential; some thing that covers your ears and again of the neck. I already had a North Face one, which I used. A heat beanie might be right enough.

Buff

Originally designed as headwear, humans frequently use them in different approaches consisting of neck scarves, handkerchiefs and mouth coverings for while the path receives dusty. See the demo on their internet site for a myriad of approaches wherein to apply one. Light sufficient for weight now no longer to be an issue.

Toilet roll

Toilet roll isn't provided in maximum centers in Nepal so that you should offer your own. Not to worry - you could purchase unmarried rolls pretty much anywhere. It's very reasonably-priced so now no longer really well worth bringing from your own home country. Buy a roll in Kathmandu to get you commenced and fill up as wished alongside they manner.

Travel towel

Microfibre tour towels are lighter, extra absorbent and lots extra compact than regular towels. I sold mine on Amazon from a organization referred to as Starwood Sports and became very satisfied with it.

Water purification system

The water in Nepal has usually been a piece dodgy for Westerners to drink and have to in no way be under the influence of alcohol directly from the faucet. Some declare you shouldn't even use it to sweep your teeth. Fortunately there are some of answers to be had for water purification.

- Bottled water
- Purification Tablets
- Boiling
- Steripen
- Water filter

Bottled water – to be had at the trek. In Kathmandu you could purchase sorts – the same old manufacturers we're all acquainted with and water that has glaringly been bottled and sealed locally. There is a sizable charge difference, with the latter costing approximately 15-20 rupees according to litre. On the trek, water receives extra highly-priced the better you go (as does the whole thing else), because it needs to be carried further. Though I've heard the Sherpas who convey it don't receives a commission an entire lot extra. Buying bottled water is seemed as ecologically unsound as there are few recycling centers withinside the Khumbu – so in case you take care of the surroundings possibly you have to preserve this to a minimum.

Water Purification Tablets – This has usually regarded like a number of problem to me. Coupled with the reality they make the water flavor vile makes me surprise why every body might trouble if there have been different alternatives to be had. Some humans propose including flavouring to dispose of the flavor, which simply looks as if extra problem. For a unmarried ride this might be the most inexpensive alternative however I might keep away from it.

Boiling – The time honoured technique of ensuring your water's secure to drink. You can ask teahouses to boil a few water to fill your bottle. Although I didn't try this I witnessed others do it. It's not unusualplace exercise at the trek, now no longer deemed uncommon in any manner and nobody bats an eye-lid.

Steripen – A battery powered tool you could use to zap your water and it kills all of the pathogens. I've in no way used one however seemingly they may be very effective. Just to confuse you, there are various sorts all doing extra or much less the identical thing. The Steripen Ultra is probably really well

worth thinking about as it could be powered via way of means of plugging right into a USB outlet. This technique is a touch highly-priced and
likely now no longer really well worth making an investment in for a unmarried ride.

Water-clear out – Attach one to the neck of a bottle and simply drink. This will filter all of the nasty stuff. Simple and effective. Long time period those exercise session inexpensive than the usage of purification tablets. I sold the Sawyer water clear out. This comes with a water pouch which attaches to the clear out or you could screw it onto any general length plastic water bottle. This method you could purchase a bottle of water, fill up it with regular faucet water to apply once more with the clear out attached, which could be very convenient. I used this every time I drank water, a few bottled, a few faucet and didn't have any problem. The pouch ripped earlier than my trek became over however that is nevertheless a good deal and the pouch seems like an useless add-on in any case.

Water bottle

Buy a 1 litre steel type, to be had from any tenting save, so you can convey boiled water.

Money belt/pouch

Besides warding off pickpockets, having a cash belt or pouch is a great concept for some of reasons. As formerly stated, there aren't anyt any coins machines past Namche so that you are going to should convey a number of coins on you. It's definitely now no longer realistic to hold all of it for your pockets so that you'll want some thing else, ideally some thing you could wear. It's now no longer an awesome concept to preserve all of your cash in a single location besides and taking your pockets out always will increase the possibilities of dropping cash. As you may have a number of big notes it's an awesome concept to save those in a cash belt, to be transferred while wished, whilst you preserve simply what you observed you're going to spend every day for your pockets.

I opted for the Bago Hidden Travel Wallet – Passport Holder RFID Safety – Neck Stash Belt Pouch. This became a touch gem and absolutely justified all of the superb critiques it gets on Amazon. It became massive sufficient to deal with my money, passport, vaccine card and permits, retaining all my necessities in a single place. Lightweight and without problems adjustable, I wore it subsequent to my frame the complete trek and didn't even note I became sporting it. I opted for the Khaki shade because it's much less probably to expose via a t-shirt. For each person strange with RFID robbery that is a technique thieves use to examine chips off contactless playing cards and passports. The Bago prevents this and seemingly it

works a treat.

Map

As each person who has been to EBC will inform you, you don't want a map to discover your manner due to the fact the path is so definitely marked. What you want a map for is making plans wherein to goal for every day earlier than you spark off and experiencing the amusing and pleasure as you attain your vacation spot and tick it off the list. I don't suppose my journey could were pretty as plenty amusing with out one. I selected the National Geographic map to EBC, which introduced on it's promise of being clean to examine, open and close, in addition to being rugged and tear-proof. Can't advocate it distinctly sufficient. Find it on Amazon for approximately a fiver.

Camera

I've visible human beings use their DSLRS, which glaringly produce beautiful pics withinside the proper hAnds. I left mine at domestic and opted as an alternative for a touch Sony DSCW800 compact. Not best did I now no longer need the fear of losing/negative my DSLR, however it became greater weight I may want to in reality do with out. I additionally appeared cameras as a non-vital object. When I cross someplace I need to enjoy it at the same time as I'm there, now no longer once I get domestic. The Sony became mild sufficient now no longer to be an problem and took high-quality pics. And, notwithstanding what I've simply said, for the primary time in my lifestyles I discovered myself taking too many.

It's a touch impolite to head round pointing cameras at human beings, and maximum travelogues rightly endorse asking their permission first. The problem with this, as I discovered extra than once, is that they will be inclined to say 'No'. After some time you could discover your self wishing you hadn't asked. One manner to get round that is to take their picturegraph with out their understanding. Ensure your lens is on a wide- attitude setting – then, in preference to pointing the digital digicam immediately at them, goal it toward some thing else nearby. The actual situation of your picturegraph might be withinside the body with out their understanding and you'll discover your pics are better, for the reason that you may be the usage of the 'rule of thirds', in preference to constantly having your situation useless centre. Devious? Amoral? What the hell – nobody died.

Khumbu kids - two completely willing subjects on this occasion.

E-Reader

There might be instances while solo trekking, while you may be in your very own and can require a few shape of entertainment. It receives darkish pretty early in Nepal. Teahouses frequently close up save quickly after dinner and exhausted trekkers drag themselves off to mattress round 9 o'clock. You might not need to visit your room and stare at 4 partitions for multiple hours earlier than in the end nodding off, so having some thing to examine is a superb idea. We're lucky to stay withinside the age of Kindle, because of this that now no longer having to haul a load of paperbacks throughout continents, wherein there can be an absence of English language fabric available (aleven though now no longer in Nepal, I may upload).

I delivered my iPad mini with me – virtually due to the fact that's what I already had. However iPads, even minis, are a touch heavy so I could propose shopping for a reasonably-priced Kindle reader (with net capabilities) to hold the burden down. You may want to of route virtually use your smartphone, however the batteries on those lessen plenty faster than an e-reader.

Solar charger

This is one object I'm extraordinarily satisfied I delivered, permitting me to fee my gadgets as I walked, on the equal time fending off paying charging fees on the lodges (they could quick upload up).

Many sun chargers I checked out on Amazon had an uncomfortably excessive ratio of bad to superb critiques – some thing I by no means like because it way simply having to take a chance. Like maximum human beings looking for a sun charger, I became tempted with the aid of using the cool - sounding however highly-priced Goal Zero range. In the stop I determined to head for the much less high priced PortaPow 11w Rainproof Dual USB Solar Charger. Rainproof is vital for apparent reasons (aleven though they almost all are) and having USB ports intended I may want to fee my digital digicam and iPad on the equal time. I became involved 11w wouldn't be effective sufficient to lend good sized fee to the iPad however it became fine.

I get the impact that a excessive percentage of the terrible critiques are left through individuals who strive the use of sun chargers withinside the cloudy UK and are upset with the results. In Nepal this wasn't a hassle because it changed into sunny almost all the time. Securing your sun charger to the returned of your rucksack method it could trickle fee your gadgets as you walk. Find the pleasant manner to do that earlier than you go away for Nepal and don't do as I did and battle with it even as you're at the trek. I have to upload right here that I changed into taken aback at how rapid the PortaPow charged up my Sony digital digicam from 0 to full. It changed into in all likelihood as powerful as plugging it right into a strength outlet. No kidding.

Travel adapter

Check out this reachable journey adapter with connections for 4 USB gadgets. If this doesn't contend with your charging necessities not anything will

And for pretty much all of your journey techie desires a domain properly really well worth a go to is Too Many Adapters -

Head-torch

The lighting exit pretty early withinside the Khumbu region. You'll want a head-torch for the ones overdue night time lavatory trips (whenever after 9pm) in a few teahouses.

Another purpose to have a head-torch is withinside the occasion you're silly sufficient to hold hiking after dark. This is how I ended up napping out on my manner returned to Lukla. I began out off from Gorak Shep withinside the morning, assembly with the same old crowds of yak trains and different trekkers that could make it gradual going even if headed returned down. Before lengthy the crowds began out to skinny and shortly I changed into on a roll, on foot hours with out seeing every other human being, relishing the solitude and feeling extra energised than I'd felt in days. I had firstly meant to prevent at Pangboche, that's thirds of the manner returned to Namche and a great day's trek. But once I were given there early night it changed into nonetheless pretty mild and my legs simply didn't need to prevent on foot. So I appeared at the map and determined I should make it to Tengboche with one remaining push. And on I went. Soon the solar began out taking place and earlier than lengthy I needed to take out my head-torch. Shortly after that even the ones few stragglers who have been nonetheless at the trek began out disappearing till I changed into all on my own. I don't understand how I misplaced my manner exactly – all I understand is that I got here throughout a big boulder that changed into impassable. That changed into once I realised I wasn't at the EBC path anymore. I became round to head returned the manner I got here – however now even that wasn't clear. My head-torch threw no extra than more than one toes of mild in the front of me. To both aspect have been drop-offs and I didn't have sufficient mild to inform in the event that they have been toes or twenty toes. No longer relishing the solitude, I realised I had painted myself right into a nook and through going everywhere I changed into risking falling and breaking a leg – or worse. I don't thoughts admitting I were given quite freaked out for a even as. That is till I realised my pleasant choice changed into to live positioned till morning, as unappealing because it seemed. At 6pm I knew I had an extended night time beforehand however I were given into my napping bag and hunkered down. I took out my iPad and examine for a even as, taking note of the sounds of the Himalayas, thankful that the nearby animal populace doesn't consist of bears and wolves. For basically anecdotal functions I would love to have the ability to mention there has been a typhoon that night time and I slightly survived. But the fact is it changed into one of the maximum fine nights I spent at the trek. The brush I lay throughout changed into like a springy bed masking up the tough ground. And whilst the cloud cowl cleared I changed into greeted with a celeb stuffed sky the like of which I've seldom seen. I drifted inside and outside of sleep in the course of the night time, imagining at the primary mild of sunrise I might be up and gone. But I neglected sunrise entirely, laying in till approximately 8 a.m., ultimately waking up included in sweat.

Later I associated this tale to a Sherpa who predictably stated "You have to have had a guide". "You might say that", I informed him and he laughed.

The lesson right here is to prevent hiking earlier than dark. The irony, of course, is if I hadn't introduced a head-torch I wouldn't have even tried it – however that's no purpose now no longer to convey a head-torch.

First Aid Kit

Try now no longer to get carried away - only a few fundamentals you may want. Sticking plasters, Diamox, Paracetamol, Imodium Dioralyte. It's not going you'll use the whole contents of a box (e.g. 30 paracetamol), until you're definitely unfortunate. Don't convey the packing containers both – empty the contents right into a small ziplock bag or similar. Ideally you have to be capable of squeeze this lot right into a aspect pocket of your rucksack.

Chapstick

I didn't use this kind of and sorely regretted it. I've by no means a great deal suffered from chapped lips, however right here I did. It turned into pretty close to the give up of my trek, however didn't resolve till once I were given domestic.

Suncream

I added this, forgot to apply it on more than one activities and sorely regretted it. Sunburn creeps up on you. I continually overlook the way you don't note it going on till it's too past due. Bring a few and don't overlook to apply it.

Pocket Ashtray Pouch

I'm proud to mention I didn't drop a unmarried cigarette butt withinside the Khumbu location way to my trusty cigarette pouch. These may be picked up pretty affordably on Amazon or Bay.

Earplugs

You'll discover those beneficial if staying in Thamel, wherein pubs and golf equipment play eighties rock tune past due into the night. Depending on which airline you fly with you could discover a pair withinside the little goody bag they supply.

Packing your sleeping bag

Your sound asleep bag might be the bulkiest object you're going to be sporting so the higher you compress it down the extra room you'll have on your rucksack for different essentials. Use a compression stuff sack as opposed to doing struggle with the usual one which got here together along with your bag. Stuff the bag into the stuff sack with the aid of using the tail give up, as opposed to hood first. This allows the air to get away thru the open give up as you compress it down, rather than turning into trapped withinside the foot box. Hold the stuff sack among your knees and twist it round as you push the bag internal. Another aspect that allows is to show the bag internal out. The wind resistant cloth on many luggage does a first rate task of preserving out the bloodless however it therefore traps air internal, making luggage blow up like a balloon as you attempt to squeeze them down – turning internal out allows keep away from this.

Packing your rucksack

It's now no longer like packing a box, wherein it typically makes feel to place the heaviest objects to the lowest. Lighter objects need to be positioned at the lowest and heavier objects on the pinnacle, near your returned so that they take a seat down among your shoulder blades. This locations maximum of the burden in your hips taking the stress off your shoulders. Conveniently, one of the lighter objects could be your sound asleep bag, that you best want to take out ultimate aspect at night. Put this in first and construct on it, setting objects you could want short get right of entry to to close to the pinnacle to keep away from having to drag out the entirety else to get to them. Some rucksacks have an good sized quantity of wallet and it's smooth to overlook wherein you've positioned objects, so get withinside the addiction of returning objects to the identical pocket you took them from and you'll quickly start to memorise wherein the entirety is.

YouTube is your friend. Check out the numerous films on how satisfactory to percent a rucksack earlier than you leave.

Preparation Checklist

- Buy return ticket to Kathmandu
- Make doctor appointment to obtain vaccines and buy Diamox

- Obtain 30 day visa (or wait until you get there)
- Reserve hostel or hotel in Thamel, Kathmandu online if insecure about just turning up
- Buy travel insurance – trekking above 5000m (+ helicopter rescue)
- Contact your bank to inform travel dates
- Book one-way ticket to Lukla online
- Buy/bring US dollars for return leg of Luka flight, visa and standard spending money
- Obtain passport photos for visa/permits/sim card
- Check in online
- Arrive Kathmandu
- Begin taking Diamox
- Buy local sim card (passport + photo needed)
- Exchange enough currency for duration of trek (passport needed)
- Obtain necessary permits. (passport + photos needed)
- Fly to Lukla

Arriving in Kathmandu

If you haven't already obtained a visa, you'll, along side maximum humans in your aircraft, want to fill out an software shape after you've surpassed thru security. This is while you'll want you'd added a pen, and be trying to find a few type soul to speedy fill out their shape and lend you theirs, forcing them to attend as a way to fill out yours for you to get on with their holiday. So carry a reasonably-priced Biro so that it will keep away from this, and heroically hand it to a person else while you're performed. The passport images you added with you'll prevent the time and fee of getting them performed right here, permitting you to speedy be a part of the road and get your visa. Remember you'll want to pay in greenbacks. Those those who had the foresight to attain their visas earlier than leaving domestic could be

looking ahead to you on the bags carousel while you arrive. Waiting in your bags to get off the aircraft can take one to 1 and a 1/2 of hours. That's approximately how lengthy I waited and I spoke to those who instructed me it isn't always unusual. Ignore everyone supplying you a luggage trolley as there's a price for this after you get outside. In fact, most often of thumb, forget about everyone supplying you some thing you don't really need or want or should in any other case attain your self with minimum effort.

After you've picked up your luggage you'll need to get a taxi for your lodge or hostel in Thamel. Before you do, discover a currency trading withinside the airport and extrade as small quantity of forex as possible. Currency exchanges in airports provide notoriously horrific change quotes and truely need to be prevented the sector over. Ten greenbacks could be extra than sufficient to cowl the taxi fare and purchase you more than one cups of espresso till you discover an change in Thamel supplying a ways higher quotes. Don't worry – there are lots.

You'll locate an authentic Airport taxi provider table at the left as you close to the go out doors. This is barely extra costly than the handfuls of taxi drivers ready outdoor the airport doors, clamouring on your custom. It's a buyer's marketplace so don't be afraid to haggle. Even at inflated costs the price of a taxi into Thamel is subsequent to not anything as compared to what you'll pay withinside the West so don't haggle too hard - those men have were given to earn a living. If you're some thing like me, you'll haggle due to the fact you sense you've got got to, then supply the driving force a tip, bringing the overall fare to extra than he requested for withinside the first region.

If you've never been to a third world country before (and even if you have), the taxi ride from the airport into Thamel is very exciting. Personally I love the chaos and vibrant street life that is the antithesis of comparatively clean and controlled European cities. By the way - be aware when crossing the street in Kathmandu, zebra crossings are really only there to decorate the road.

TO DO IN KATHMANDU

It could be loopy to move all of the manner to Kathmandu with out spending a while taking withinside the city's delights both earlier than or after your EBC trek. Getting round is quality executed with the aid of using taking walks or getting a taxi. If staying in Thamel, you'll locate the crowded dusty streets can all appearance pretty similar, making it very
clean to lose your bearings. An effortlessly recognisable landmark is the well-known Kathmandu Guesthouse, which stands at a junction wherein you could effortlessly orient your self to anywhere else. It is proper contrary the

Thamel supermarket, a fave trekker/traveller one-forestall save for stocking up on supplies. If you're confined on time right here are some ought to sees.

Durbar Square

Located simply south of Thamel, that is a UNESCO international background web website online and Kathmandu's fundamental traveller attraction. While there may be no price for locals, vacationers ought to pay 1000NR for an afternoon price price tag to go into the rectangular. There are little price price tag cubicles at every front to the rectangular – attempt accidently taking walks beyond and you'll be in a well mannered way referred to as returned with the aid of using the high-quality guy inside. With your price price tag you'll be given a reachable little e-book with a map/manual to all of the homes withinside the rectangular. The front charge has quadrupled in latest years to the dismay of a few and aleven though the rectangular suffered tremendous earthquake damage, it's nonetheless properly really well worth a go to.

If you're going to be staying in Kathmandu some time remember getting a Durbar Square visitor's byskip for no greater price. You'll want your passport and a pair of passport photos – get your price price tag from the sales space then head to the price price tag workplace subsequent to Kumari House to choose up an ID card. NOTE – you ought to stroll right here via the vintage town, for a captivating flavor of Kathmandu road-lifestyles.

Kal Bhairab in Durbar Square.

Swayambhunath (The Monkey Temple)

This is a superb distance from Thamel, excessive up on a hill, observed with the aid of using 365 steps to the top – so in case you're quick on time or want to preserve your electricity for hiking I could advise getting a taxi. Entrance charge is two hundred rupees, (loose for locals) and the monkeys are a delight. Just don't try and feed them. It has a top notch series of shrines and stupas, and extraordinary perspectives of Kathmandu.

Boudhanath

Sadly the stupa at Boudhanath took a hammering throughout the earthquake, however is presently being rebuilt. You can go to any time of day, however get right here withinside the mornings to look the clergymen stroll across the prayer wheels – and be a part of in in case you want. Entrance is 250 rupees.

The stupa at Boudhanath, currently undergoing repair.

The Garuda Hotel

For Everest junkies, or people with even a passing hobby in mountaineering, pop into the Garuda Hotel in Thamel. On the partitions going up the steps are snap shots and mementos from a number of the top notch Everest expeditions who've stayed right here. At one time this changed into the visit region for climbers. The 1996 Adventure Consultants Everest day trip stayed right here, that is why it changed into of hobby to me. I stayed for 3 nights on my go back from Base Camp. The not unusualplace regions now have a dwindled grandeur harking back to the vintage resorts on the incorrect facet of the Las Vegas strip, however the rooms are smooth and bright. (Rooms are $15-20 in line with night). The personnel are very pleasant and had been extraordinarily useful once I discovered myself rupeeless, having been refused cash from 3 ATMs. They permit me use their mobileular telecellsmartphone to name my UK financial institution and didn't even price me for the price of the call – a very good twenty mins at the telecellsmartphone. As it grew to become out, in spite of having knowledgeable them I could be in Nepal, a be aware hadn't been placed on my account and the cardboard changed into blocked. This changed into quick amended. And I certain changed into thankful to the hotel.

NOTE – for an intensive study getting the high-quality out of Kathmandu, consisting of locations to devour and stay, you can't do higher than go to travel

FLYING TO LUKLA

You can ee-e book your Lukla flight on line earlier than leaving home. You shouldn't ee-e book a go back flight as you can't be simply positive what date you'll be flying back. The unforeseeable can take place which means you want to go back in advance or later than expected. Lukla flights are infamous for being cancelled because of awful climate and it's been recognised for human beings to loaf around for days.

The biggest flight operator is Tara Air. Though there are some of others the fares are all quite a whole lot the same. One cause a few human beings nonetheless pick out to trek all of the manner from Jiri is that Tenzig-Hilary Airport in Lukla has a popularity as one of, if now no longer the maximum risky airport withinside the world. This is essentially due to its very brief sloping runway, which culminates in a cliff.

Flights to Lukla leave best withinside the morning so that you will want to upward thrust early and get a taxi to the airport, permitting sufficient time to test in. You will find clumps of taxi drivers parked in the streets around Thamel waiting for your custom at all hours but if you're worried about finding a taxi that early in the morning ask your hotel to order one the night before. If the motel calls for fee for the taxi ensure your driving force is aware of you've got got already paid earlier than you get withinside the car. I suffered a small conversation breakdown among the motel and taxi driving force, which nearly led to me having to pay twice!

The flights are on the ones little propeller planes, similar to withinside the antique movies – it's all very romantic. Some pointers:

- Listen carefully for your flight to be called – it's all mumbles over the PA. In fact use all of your available senses to determine when your flight is due
- You can't take any baggage on with you – check it all in. You'll get a little ticket, which you use to collect it at the other side
- There are no seat numbers – you just get on the plane and find a seat
- For the best views sit on the left side of the plane on the journey out. Lots of other tourists will have heard about this too and will be trying to do the same. Don't get hung up about it if you miss the chance. The views are nice, but nothing compared to what's to follow once you land

9 Day Itinerary

I had no constant itinerary in thoughts after I set out (aside from understanding I might in all likelihood be acclimatising in Namche), and I encompass the subsequent best to offer a hard evaluation of the viable alternatives. I haven't protected popular estimates on how lengthy it takes to get from factor A to factor B, as I assume they're deceptive and serve little purpose. Such estimates fail to account for basics like preventing for lunch, take day trip to virtually loosen up and experience the scenery, or chat to fellow trekkers.

Day 1: Lukla – Phakding

Day 2: Phakding – Namche

Day 3: ACCLIMATISATION day at Namche

Day 4: Namche – Tengboche

Day 5: Tengboche – Dingboche

Day 6: ACCLIMATISATION day at Dingboche

Day 7: Dingboche – Lobuche

Day 8: Lobuche – Gorak Shep

Day 9: Gorak Shep to Kala Patar and EBC

This itinerary guarantees you've got got a incredibly smooth first day. I understand I'm now no longer on my own in wondering that the toughest a part of the whole trek is from the double suspension bridges as much as Namche - a chain of stone steps that appear to move on forever. Many human beings opt to keep on foot to Monjo on day 1 to make day 2 a bit easier (aleven though now no longer a whole lot). Whichever you pick out, the coolest information is if you're robust sufficient to attain Namche, the toughest element is at the back of you (Any issues you've got got from right here are much less possibly to do with health than

how properly you acclimatise). I stayed in Phakding – however if I needed to do it once more I might honestly push myself and intention for Monjo. Getting to Phakding took me six hours. Though to be truthful I had pulled a muscle in my calf. How did I manipulate that? Okay, right here's the element approximately human beings of a positive age - you don't simply should do lots in an effort to injure yourself. I can injure myself mendacity in bed. And so it turned into that I turned into on foot along, approximately an hour out of Lukla after I pulled a muscle in my calf. It wasn't precisely suffering however nonetheless painful sufficient that I needed to limp the relaxation of the manner to Phakding. As it transpired, this did now no longer cross unnoticed. A few trekkers expressed their admiration that I turned into decided to hold on in spite of my apparent obstacle and shortly I even commenced to experience a bit heroic. The following morning I turned into even mildly disillusioned to awaken and find out my leg turned into best once more and nowadays I might be simply any other trekker and now no longer the heroic man with the limp. Yep, that's how unhappy I am.

For the ones driven for time it's miles viable to upward thrust early and climb Kala Patar to peer the sunrise. You can then go back to Gorak Shep for breakfast (or lunch) and visit Base Camp withinside the afternoon.

Twin suspension bridges below Namche. The good news is you get to go along the top one.

10 Day Itinerary

Day 1: Lukla – Monjo

Day 2: Monjo – Namche

Day 3: ACCLIMATISATION day at Namche

Day 4: Namche – Tengboche

Day 5: Tengboche – Pheriche

Day 6: ACCLIMATISATION day at Pheriche

Day 7: Pheriche – Lobuche

Day 8: Lobuche – Gorak Shep

Day 9: Gorak Shep – EBC

Day 10: Gorak Shep – Kala Patar

As already outlined, a key distinction goes that little bit similarly to attain Monjo on Day 1, making day 2 barely easier. This doesn't imply you have to try and cross similarly than Namche on day 3. Namche is the best vicinity to acclimatise in addition to meet different trekkers and simply hold out.

Instead of seeking to do Kala Patar and Base Camp on day 9, visit Base

Camp first, get a few nicely earned relaxation and upward thrust early for Kala Patar the subsequent morning. You'll be returned with lots of time to have lunch in Gorak Shep and begin trekking returned down.

TRAIL FEATURES

You'll meet many Yak trains and their handlers alongside the manner. It's clever to prevent and allow them to byskip at the out of doors because it's been recognised for trekkers to be by accident shoved over the threshold of the precipice. Depending on wherein it occurs the outcomes can variety from humiliating to fatal. It's without a doubt top manners to prevent and allow Sherpas suffering with heavy hundreds byskip in any respect times.

Donkeys are a less common site than yaks. But this photo illustrates why you should let all animals pass on the outside.

Ubiquitous capabilities of the trek are the lovely Mani stones and prayer wheels. Tradition calls for you live to the left whilst passing, however don't fear in case you forget – no one's going to leap out at you. Spin the prayer wheels clockwise as you byskip.

Stay to the left of Mani stones and prayer wheels.

Suspension bridges

Those with a worry of heights can be in for a difficult time. There are severa suspension bridges alongside the manner, spanning the Dudh Kosi, a quick flowing river that runs nearly the whole period of the trek. Some of them are pretty excessive however I can guarantee you they experience very strong and also you by no means honestly experience like you're in any danger.

Sturdy steel suspension bridge with prayer flags.

Waterfalls

You can spend quite a few time simply preventing and watching those.

One of many beautiful waterfalls.

Recycling bins

Keep the Khumbu smooth! You'll see quite a few those lovable stone systems alongside the manner. I'm satisfied to mention the path is spotlessly smooth and trekkers appear like respecting the environment.

Recycling bins – a lot nicer than the ones at home.

TREK HIGHLIGHTS

Namche Bazaar

This is the unofficial capital of the Khumbu and an excellent vicinity to take your first acclimatisation day. Rather than simply take a seat down around, acclimatisation days have to be spent hiking a bit better than wherein you'll be sleeping, so it's an excellent concept to do a brief trek above Namche. A famous trek is to the Everest View Hotel, which, as you would possibly expect, offers extremely good perspectives of Everest. Nearby are the picturesque villages of Khumjung and Khunde, each really well worth a go to.

If you're now no longer feeling highly energetic, an opportunity is to stroll as much as Syangboche airstrip. This is extra like a bit of barren wasteground than an airstrip and, I'm told, is handiest honestly utilized by helicopters; but it offers extremely good perspectives of Namche.

Namche in pefect weather.

A first-class manner to whittle away an hour or is to go to the Sherpa Museum. It offers an perception into Sherpa way of life in addition to Everest history. If you knew not anything approximately Everest you will be forgiven for questioning Sir Edmund Hillary turned into the handiest man or woman ever to climb the mountain, as there may be little else approximately different Western climbers. The overdue Sir Edmund is some thing of a close to god in those parts, deservedly so for the exceptional paintings he did for the place over many decades.

The Sherpa Museum. There's no photography allowed, I learned after taking this.

If you occur to discover your self in Namche on a Saturday an appeal is the weekly marketplace wherein many Sherpas and shopkeepers meet to alternate goods. At any time you may inventory up on the ones forgotten gadgets or snacks, which get extra luxurious as you get similarly up the path. Namche is likewise a extremely good vicinity to shop for souvenirs for the peoples returned home, aleven though glaringly you have to go away this type of buying till you're in your manner returned down.

If you've completed your acclimatisation trek and are searching out some thing else to hold you occupied multiple the bars display mountain climbing movies at 3pm. I watched a pair and it's now no longer almost as uninteresting because it sounds, I promise.

I endorse staying at the least one night time withinside the Khumbu Lodge, which has been the Namche HQ for lots extremely good Everest expeditions, which include the 1996 expedition – so certainly it turned into part of my 'Into Thin Air' pilgrimage. As you'd expect, some of images decorate the partitions from many expeditions – however there may be one which honestly sticks out a few of the others. As you stroll via the the front door, at once at the proper is a framed picturegraph of Robert Redford, with Namche withinside the background. I suppose what befell is Redford got here to metropolis and nobody idea to get a picturegraph of him on the time -

so a person with fundamental Photoshop abilities determined to position matters proper.

A room right here with connected rest room will set you again $20 whilst one with out a rest room may be had for $2. All the rooms have little brass plaques at the doorways with the names of climbers who've stayed there. I located myself withinside the 'David Breashears' room on each my visits. Breashears is a climber/filmmaker who become at the mountain in 'ninety six to make an IMAX film for the National Geographic channel. He become at Base Camp because the tragedy opened up and assisted withinside the rescue effort.

This vicinity would possibly simply have the most important not unusualplace room/eating place withinside the Khumbu and withinside the night is humming with different trekkers of all ages. In one nook is a great library of mountain climbing books to read. If you're like me you'll be salivating over them.

It become withinside the Khumbu Lodge I met a nineteen yr antique Aussie referred to as Monte, who become hiking to Base Camp together along with his dad, John, in addition to tackling some peaks withinside the region. Both had walked all of the manner from Jiri and had been cause on tenting out at Base Camp.

"You imply you've added a tent?" I asked.

'Yes', stated Monte.

"Wow, I really need to live at Base Camp too. I'll provide you $one hundred in case you allow me proportion it. Oh… there likely isn't room. What length tent is it?"

Monte concept approximately it a second then replied: "It's a 3 guy tent".

Perfect, I concept. I become going to get an possibility to sleep at Base Camp after all. And thinking about this younger man had hauled his tent all of the manner from Jiri I felt it become a quite correct deal. Monte delivered that he might need to k it together along with his dad first, however might allow me understand.

Tengboche

This tiny village is quality recognized for its stunning monastery. You can stroll round or even meditate with the clergymen in case you experience so inclined. Prayers are held two times a day – five am for early risers and 3pm for the relaxation of us. Tengboche additionally takes place to provide marvelous perspectives of Everest, Ama Dablam, Lhotse and Nuptse to call some. There's a massive inn referred to as Hotel Himalayan proper contrary the monastery. I didn't live right here, however multiple individuals who did knowledgeable me that it value one hundred rupees, that is similar to you'll pay withinside the small lodges. They concept it become a high-quality vicinity to live additionally, with super perspectives.

The monastery in Tengboche.

Dingboche and Pheriche

If you examine a EBC map you'll see that across the half-manner mark the course diverges, supplying you with a preference of going in the direction of Dingboche or Pheriche. The female proprietor of the hotel wherein I stayed in Tengboche cautioned me to keep away from Pheriche, as it's lots less warm and windier than Dingboche, so I accompanied her advice. I exceeded fast thru Pheriche on my manner again down, and I assume she become proper. As properly as being a bit warmer, Dingboche has a steep hill you could climb to your acclimatisation hike. There are a few high-quality perspectives from the pinnacle furnished you rise up early earlier than the mist descends. When it does, it's a piece like a scene from that antique John Carpenter film 'The Fog'. I stayed withinside the Snowlion Lodge, that is the primary one you return back to while getting into the village and which I can recommend. They offer satisfactory at ease rooms, correct food, and actually have their very own Facebook page. Modern times.

Pheriche is domestic to the scientific hospital of the Himalayan Rescue

Association,

best open throughout the 2 essential hiking seasons of March-May and November-December. At 3pm there's a every day communicate with the aid of using one of the medical doctors approximately the risks of altitude sickness. If you're already feeling a bit sick then heading for Pheriche is probably a smart option.

The Sherpa Memorial

Leaving Dingboche going in the direction of the village of Louboche the trek leads you up in the direction of the Sherpa memorial in Dughla Pass. This become excessive on my itinerary as I supposed to go to the memorial to Scott Fischer, one of the publications who died on that fateful day in 1996. And so on twelfth October 2015 I reached the pinnacle of the promontory wherein the webweb page is situated. As I stopped to

capture my breath I observed a younger couple, in matching blue down jackets, a brief distance away to my proper, with a Sherpa manual nearby. I took them to be different trekkers and moved toward see which of the memorials they had been studying. As it grew to become out, it become the Scott Fischer memorial. I stood with them a bit whilst and it quickly have become obvious the female become crying. I regarded round, wondering right here become a person even extra moved with the aid of using the tragedy than I become. When the female regarded again I felt pressured to mention something.

"I understand what you imply," become the quality I should muster up.

She gave me a bit smile, and replied, "He become our Dad. This is our first time right here".

With that Katie Fischer brought herself and her brother Andy, even as my mind attempted to compute the truth that I had arrived at Scott Fischer's memorial on the equal time as his grown up children, nineteen years after his demise. At that moment, with the type of uncanny timing seldom determined outdoor a Hollywood movie, it started to snow. (I'm now no longer making this up).

"It's snowing", Katie observed.

"Jesus, that's appropriate", I replied, possibly inappropriately. Then added: "Look, I'm simply going to present you a while through yourselves", and scuttled off.

Low-mendacity cloud obscured the encompassing panorama and shortly a kick back wind whipped up, sending the snow careening throughout the Dughla Pass. A small scattering of traffic attended the alternative memorials to fallen climbers in what made for a completely bleak scene. It jogged my memory of Sunday cemetery journeys as a infant to place flora on graves of human beings I'd in no way even met.

I watched for some time from a distance as Katie and Andy located stones on their dad's memorial, sharing hugs, tears and low laughter. I saved replaying her phrases in my head "He changed into our Dad. This is our first time here." and earlier than I knew it I changed into crying too.

Andy and Katie place stones on their father's memorial.

I dried my eyes and again after approximately fifteen minutes. I determined myself looking to invite questions and now no longer understanding what inquiries to ask, unprepared as I changed into for this event. I additionally knew it changed into neither the time nor the vicinity despite the fact that I did. The ultimate aspect they wished changed into a few type of bizarre fan-boy haranguing them approximately their father's demise. Nevertheless, I informed them why I had come to Nepal and that I changed into acquainted with Scott Fischer's story. They thanked me for honouring him through coming to the memorial.

Before leaving I informed them I concept their father changed into an extremely good man, now no longer actually to be kind, however due to the fact he changed into. Scott Fischer changed into recognized for his ascents of a number of the best mountains on earth, with out the usage of supplemental oxygen. Before his demise he had placed in the back of him six of the 'seven summits', the best mountains on every of the seven continents. This covered K2, the 'mountaineer's mountain', extensively appeared because the most difficult of them all.

Gorak Shep

It is the ultimate bastion of civilisation earlier than Base Camp. It is probably deceptive to name it a village, comprising, because it does, multiple motels and some outhouses. There are almost as many ponies as there are residents. I stayed withinside the Snowland Highest Inn, that's a heat and inviting status quo with super meals and outstanding atmosphere. I ran into Monte who stated he'd okayed it together along with his dad (who I'd met fleetingly in Dingboche) and I should proportion their tent at Base Camp if I nonetheless desired to. He gave me a hard concept what time they could be getting there day after today and we organized to satisfy up.

The aptly named Snowland Highest Inn, Gorak Shep.

Outside the resort I ran into Andy and Katie again. This time we discussed 'Into Thin Air' and Andy informed me he didn't swallow Jon Krakauer's model of events. This didn't come as a great deal of a surprise. After Krakauer again to americaA and posted his piece for Outside mag he acquired a torrent of indignant letters, together with a especially scathing one from

Scott Fischer's sister. In it she condemns his complaint of numerous individuals, accusing him of being judgemental, arrogant, egotistic, and of indulging in hypothesising and tittle-tattle. Krakauer's leader complaint became directed at Anatoli Bookreev, an elite Russian mountaineer employed through Fischer as a manual. Bookreev's non-public choice to manual with out using supplemental oxygen became itself a bone of contention, and now no longer most effective with Krakauer. Although Bookreev became himself able to hiking Everest with out supplemental oxygen, many felt that during his function as a manual he ought to have used it, as is popular exercise amongst expert mountain publications. But Bookreev's choice, after having summited, to go away customers at the mountain and go back to Camp Four is what virtually drew Krakauer's condemnation. Bookreev might later try to justify his actions, claiming that Fischer gave him permission to descend in advance of his customers 'for you to make tea for them and offer aid below'. It is hardly ever being essential of Fischer to take a look at that once using Bookreev he might also additionally have made a terrible choice. Fischer selected one of the most powerful climbers withinside the global and couldn't probably have regarded how Bookreev might behave. Krakauer additionally offers Bookreev his due, concerning how the Russian courageously went out on my own into the typhoon and stored lives, even as he himself lay in his tent, exhausted and not able to assist. Far from being egotistic, the ee-e book at instances reads like a confessional, as Krakauer attempts to return back to phrases with survivor guilt and private failings. It is really well worth noting that even as Scott Fischer and one in all his publications perished at the mountain that day, none in their customers did. Sadly Bookreev became to die a 12 months later even as hiking Annapurna.

The porles of Gorak Shep.

Of Scott Fischer himself, Krakauer efficaciously portrays a rounded character. Fischer had earned himself a recognition as a wild guy who frequently threw warning to the wind, in large part because of a chain of falls from which he'd sustained accidents but brushed himself off and carried on hiking. Less properly regarded, aleven though touched on through Krakauer, is he became one of the few mountaineers who blended hiking with a social conscience. In 1996, simply months earlier than he died, Fischer led a collection up Kilimanjaro, elevating over $500 000 for the global charity company CARE (Cooperative for American Relief Everywhere). Prior to that he climbed Denali to elevate price range for Aids research. In 1994 he participated in a clean-up of Everest which became fast turning into a cesspit of empty oxygen bottles and rubbish left in the back of through severa expeditions.

Krakauer is extra essential of Adventure Consultants' owner/manual, Rob Hall, if certainly it could be termed complaint. Not with out evidence, Krakauer surmises the contention among Hall and Fischer became a issue that led Hall to make errors he won't in any other case have. The truth that errors have been made is past question. In retaining together along with his function as a journalist, Krakaeur asks why they have been made. Although the guys have been friends, Hall known the appearance of Fischer's company, Mountain Madness, on Everest as a threat

to his own, extra hooked up outfit. Adventure Consultants became till then the chief in business expeditions, placing extra customers at the summit than all and sundry else. In 1995, however, Hall had did not get a unmarried consumer to the pinnacle of Everest. He knew it became a overall performance he couldn't find the money for to repeat. In preceding years Hall had set a stringent turnaround time of 2pm for his customers and by no means swayed from it. This furnished a protection margin, permitting sufficient time for customers to descend earlier than dark, or earlier than they have been definitely too exhausted to make it again down. In exercise this intended customers, who had paid Hall up to $65, 000 to assist them attain the summit, have been pressured to show again

whether or not that they'd summited or now no longer. On tenth May 1996 Hall seemed to desert this rule. According to Krakauer a hard and fast turnaround time changed into by no means spoken approximately. Furthermore, Hall himself reached the summit round 2pm then waited a in addition hours for the very last member of his group, Doug Hansen, to make it to the top. Unlike Hall's different clients, 40-six 12 months antique Hansen changed into now no longer a rich man. A US postal worker, he have been running extra time and saving for years to comprehend his dream. He have been on Hall's group in 1995 however Hall have been pressured to show him round simply 330 ft from the summit. Naturally, Hansen changed into devastated. In the lead as much as the 'ninety six season, Hall contacted Hansen on severa activities to persuade him to provide it any other go, supplying him a extremely discounted rate. Initially reluctant, Hansen in the end took up the offer. He had any other danger to attain the summit,

one that could possibly by no means come once more. But at 2 pm on tenth May Hansen changed into struggling. Hall uncharacteristically waited on the summit for his customer. At round 4pm Hansen in the end emerged on the summit ridge. Hall even went right all the way down to help him, setting an arm round Hansen and supporting him up the very last 40 ft to the top. To say this changed into towards Hall's higher judgement might be an understatement. Krakauer speculates that Hall simply didn't have it in him to show his customer round a 2nd time. After a minute or at the summit the guys headed returned down. But Hansen had used up each ounce of electricity he had left and changed into now absolutely debilitated and not able to move. With the hurricane raging round them at the summit ridge, Hall radioed down withinside the wish of having a few bottled oxygen despatched up. This proved impossible. It changed into clean to the ones at Base Camp that there has been no wish for Doug Hansen and it changed into all Hall may want to do to store himself. But Hall refused to go away his customer notwithstanding constant urging from below. Hall's very own situation fast commenced to become worse. In a chain of transmissions that carried on in the course of the night time Hall knowledgeable his group that his fingers had been frostbitten and his legs

not worked. It seemed he changed into additionally tormented by hypoxia, his phrases turning into slurred and more and more more confused, at one factor stating: "Harold changed into with me final night time, however he doesn't look like with me now. He changed into very weak". Then moments later: "Was Harold with me? Can you inform me that?" When requested approximately Hansen he surely spoke back changed into "Doug is gone".

A rescue strive changed into made via way of means of Sherpas the subsequent morning, however
deserted because of worsening conditions. After in addition tries to speak Hall down failed, a satellite tv for pc name changed into positioned thru to his wife, Jan Arnold in Christchurch, New Zealand. Arnold, herself a mountaineer, had summited Everest in 1993 with Hall and might probable had been there once more besides for the reality she changed into seven months pregnant. She knew in addition to each person simply what her husband ought to be going thru. In a heart-wrenching trade Arnold and Hall attempted to reassure every different that each one might quit well. His very last phrases to her had been: "I love you. Sleep well, my sweetheart. Please don't fear too a good deal."

Rob Hall spent extra than 24 hours in sub-0 temperatures, struggling frostbite and with out supplemental oxygen earlier than departing this earth. His frame changed into discovered twelve days later, at the South Summit. There changed into no signal of Doug Hansen.

Everest - cold and unforgiving.

It ultimately became clear to Krakauer and others involved that day that the primary reason for so many deaths was not the storm or the actions (or inaction) of any individual but the amount of people trying to climb Everest all at the same time, forming a bottleneck on the Hilary Step that supposed climbers needed to wait in line, a few for so long as hours. This triggered many climbers to be at the mountain a good deal longer than necessary. Given that bottled oxygen isn't always inexhaustible and the way fast thoughts and frame become worse at such altitudes the outcomes aren't difficult to see. Outside mag were given the solution to their query of ways industrial expeditions had been affecting Everest, withinside the clearest terms.

Whatever trouble Andy and Katie had with Krakauer's model of events, I had no commercial enterprise debating it with them and wasn't going to try. Andy become 9 years vintage whilst his father died; Katie become five. The lack of a determine at the sort of younger age is unquantifiable. Like their father, Katie and Andy are actually concerned in charity work, presently dedicating tons in their time to elevating cash to construct colleges withinside the Khumbu place via a charity Classroom In The Clouds.

Everest Base Camp

From Gorak Shep it's far a more or less hour trek to Base Camp. There is little hazard you may be the simplest character there – and that's the first-class a part of it. Everyone who arrives is in a celebratory temper and a celebration ecosystem prevails. I had the coolest fortune to fulfill the various trekkers I had already met en route, a number of whom I'd were given to understand pretty well (and had no concept that they'd all met every different at diverse points). This is likewise while you understand why you introduced a digital digicam as you line as much as get your image taken via way of means of a fellow trekker in the front of the makeshift signal telling you you're at 5364 meters.

Finally at Everest Base Camp after nine days.

By the time I reached Base Camp and felt the temperature start to take a dive I commenced having 2nd mind approximately staying to any extent further than I wanted to. The Snowland Inn began out to appear lots cosier than it had once I left that morning. Nevertheless I felt obliged to loaf around for Monte and his dad to arrive, if simplest to inform them I'd modified my thoughts. As it become, they had been past due and I commenced to pray they wouldn't come, or at the least now no longer till after I'd gone. Having alloWed a face-saving respectful margin of time, I eventually determined they weren't coming and commenced to move back. Moments later Monte arrived, observed quickly after via way of means of John. As my thoughts wandered in the direction of a warm meal and a heat mattress, I instructed them I become having 2nd mind. John said: "Look at it this way, Graham –

how many trekkers can say they spent the night at Everest Base Camp?" At that moment I realised I would probably never get this opportunity again and was stupidly contemplating passing it up because I felt a little bit cold and tired. I said "You're right, John. What am I thinking? Let's pass". They led and I observed. John, sixty two years younger, become on his 6th day out withinside the Khumbu and had overnighted at Base Camp earlier than. He insisted the Everest signal become simplest for 'tourists', placed there via way of means of the Nepali government to forestall trekkers going any further, and that we'd should maintain on foot earlier than attending to the actual Base Camp – in which the climbers camped. We

persevered on foot for approximately every other twenty mins till eventually preventing and erecting the tent.

I have to make some thing very clear – the signal that tells 'tourists' they've reached Base Camp is there for top purpose. Beyond the signal is a treacherous panorama of boulders and fissures in which it's far all too clean to curve an ankle or damage a leg. There become little or no distance from the signal to in which we camped and I estimate if we were on foot on flat floor it might have taken no extra than multiple mins. The purpose it took goodbye is we needed to negotiate each step with terrific care. I wouldn't have dreamed of doing this by myself and I wouldn't advise you do either. I youngster you now no longer – this isn't someplace you need to be putting round after dark.

As it became out, Monte's dad become some thing of a actual lifestyles Crocodile Dundee, with years of trekking revel in and an intensive understanding of the terrific outdoors. Together they threw up the '3 guy tent' very quickly and were given the camp range going. We loved the first-class immediately noodles I've ever tasted in my lifestyles observed via way of means of mugs of warm tea simply because the mild commenced to fade. It wasn't pretty 6pm as we crawled into our slumbering bags, aware of the reality that it become a long way too early to be going to mattress however even extra aware of the plummeting temperature out of doors and the chance of wandering even some toes withinside the dark. So we lay there swapping testimonies and telling jokes, squashed collectively like sardines in a can because it dawned on me that this become now no longer as large as I'd imagined a 3 guy tent to be, not able to transport and hoping my bladder might preserve out till morning. It didn't, of course. And sooner or later withinside the night once I may want to naked it not I apologised for the disruption I become approximately to reason in clambering out to are searching for relief. John counseled me. "Don't pass anywhere. Stand on the tent flap and take a pee from there". Sound advice.

Monte fetches water from an ice cold stream for the pot.

A brief whilst later it started out to snow, lightly at first, developing gradually heavier. The snow constructed up at the partitions of the tent urgent them inwards, making it even cosier inside. Every now after which it might slide off, permitting me to respire again, at the least for a bit whilst. I could say this become the more serious night time's sleep I've ever had, if in truth I'd had any sleep. I might also additionally have dozed off for some minutes, however I can't be sure.

The subsequent morning we had been greeted through a totally special landscape. As I don't bring a thermometer I don't have any manner of understanding how bloodless it become, however approximately as bloodless as I ever need to feel. Naturally the primary aspect I had to do become to take a pee and this time I wandered a deferential distance from the tent. I positioned a foot down on what I concept become snow and watched it disappear into an ice-bloodless pool of water hid underneath. It become a second of surprise and awe; an "Oh shit!" second accompanied through an "Aw, shit" second. I despaired at what it entailed, for the reason that I had left my spare socks and different gadgets there has been no manner I may want to ever probably want again on the lodge. Fortunately John become type sufficient to provide me a spare pair, however it nonetheless took over an hour for me to get any feeling that wasn't ache again in my toes. As Monte and I sat there shivering, I couldn't assist however replicate at the truth of being out right here that no ee-e book can ever completely encapsulate. It showed for me my perception that absolutely everyone who climbs Everest, no matter revel in or lack of, no matter how a great deal cash they've or help they may want, merits a mountain of respect. The revel in highlighted for me simply how precarious and unforgiving this surroundings may be and I realised I am in reality an armchair adventurer at heart.

John made us all a warm cup of tea. We sat for some time and pointed out existence in fashionable and books in particular. John advocated a ee-e book called 'The Alchemist', which had a profound impact on him. He stated a few human beings appeared it as without a doubt a children's ee-e book, lacking the underlying message. I stated I'd appearance it up once I were given again home.

Manta and John break down the tent.

After multiple warm cups of tea we disassembled the tent and headed again to the Base Camp sign. Before we were given there we may want to listen the whoops and cheers of trekkers simply arriving. It became out to be a collection from India who ought to had been the maximum thrilled bunch of human beings I've ever met. We shared a number of their joy, taking pics and having our pics taken.

Celebrations at Base Camp

Sometime later I bid farewell to Monte and John, now no longer understanding if I'd ever see them again. As it became out, we'd pass paths on our go back to Kathmandu wherein we dined out and I had the risk to impeach Monte approximately the 3 guy tent. "Well, I may have exaggerated a bit", he laughed.

Kala Patar

This is wherein you'll get the first-rate view of Everest, simple and simple. Sadly I'm now no longer talking from private revel in. In brief – the night time with out sleep at Base Camp definitely took it out of me. I staggered again to the Snowland Inn the subsequent day, absolutely exhausted. It took me the relaxation of the day to get better and I become getting a piece bored to death of being breathless. The ultimate aspect I felt like doing become getting up early the subsequent morning to climb Kala Patar in time to look Everest at sunrise. So I lay in bed, paying attention to the sounds of hardier souls growing round 5 a.m. making ready to make what I'm advised is pretty a steep climb. I snuggled down in my sound asleep bag, just like the wuss that I am, telling myself it possibly wasn't really well worth it. That now no longer most effective had I been to Base Camp, which become my major objective, however I had stayed the night time. Do I remorse it? Hell yes! I become comforted a bit through the truth that many coming again stated cloud cowl had obscured the view and that they hadn't definitely been capable of see a great deal that morning. Later however, Alec, a Finnish man who I frolicked with in Namche on my manner down despatched me this picturegraph and I realised what I'd missed. Now I inform myself going to Kala Patar offers me a purpose to go back one day .

Everest from Kala Patar. Photograph by Alec Bergerheim.

Printed in Great Britain
by Amazon